Monologues from Shakespeare's First Folio for Women: *The Tragedies*

The Applause Shakespeare Monologue Series

Other Shakespeare Titles From Applause

Once More unto the Speech Dear Friends
Volume One: The Comedies
Compiled and Edited with Commentary by Neil Freeman

Once More unto the Speech Dear Friends
Volume Two: The Histories
Compiled and Edited with Commentary by Neil Freeman

Once More unto the Speech Dear Friends
Volume Three: The Tragedies
Compiled and Edited with Commentary by Neil Freeman

The Applause First Folio in Modern Type
Prepared and Annotated by Neil Freeman

The Folio Texts
Prepared and Annotated by Neil Freeman, Each of the 36 plays of the
Applause First Folio in Modern Type individually bound

The Applause Shakespeare Library
Plays of Shakespeare Edited for Performance

Soliloquy: The Shakespeare Monologues

Monologues from Shakespeare's First Folio for Women:
The Tragedies

Compilation and Commentary by
Neil Freeman

Edited by
Paul Sugarman

APPLAUSE
THEATRE & CINEMA BOOKS

Guilford, Connecticut

APPLAUSE
THEATRE & CINEMA BOOKS

An imprint of Globe Pequot, the trade division of
The Rowman & Littlefield Publishing Group, Inc.
4501 Forbes Blvd., Ste. 200
Lanham, MD 20706
www.rowman.com

Distributed by NATIONAL BOOK NETWORK

Library of Congress Cataloging-in-Publication Data available

Library of Congress Control Number: 2021944377

ISBN 978-1-4930-5686-6 (paperback)
ISBN 978-1-4930-5687-3 (ebook)

♾️™ The paper used in this publication meets the minimum requirements of
American National Standard for Information Sciences—Permanence of Paper for
Printed Library Materials, ANSI/NISO Z39.48-199

Dedication

Although Neil Freeman passed to that "undiscovered country" in 2015, his work continues to lead students and actors to a deeper understanding of Shakespeare's plays. With the exception of Shakespeare's words (and my humble foreword), the entirety of the material within these pages is Neil's. May these editions serve as a lasting legacy to a life of dedicated scholarship, and a great passion for Shakespeare.

Contents

FOREWORD

Paul Sugarman

Monologues from Shakespeare's First Folio presents the work of Neil Freeman, longtime champion of Shakespeare's First Folio, whose groundbreaking explorations into how first printings offered insights to the text in rehearsals, stage and in the classroom. This work continued with *Once More Unto the Speech Dear Friends: Monologues from Shakespeare's First Folio with Modern Text Versions for Comparison* where Neil collected over 900 monologues divided between the Comedy, History and Tragedy Published by Applause in three masterful volumes which present the original First Folio text side by side with the modern, edited version of the text. These volumes provide a massive amount of material and information. However both the literary scope, and the literal size of these volumes can be intimidating and overwhelming. This series' intent is to make the work more accessible by taking material from the encyclopediac original volumes and presenting it in an accessible workbook format.

To better focus the work for actors and students the texts are contrasted side by side with introductory notes before and commentary after to aid the exploration of the text. By comparing modern and First Folio printings, Neil points the way to gain new insights into Shakespeare's text. Editors over the centuries have "corrected" and updated the texts to make them "accessible," or "grammatically correct." In doing so they have lost vital clues and information that Shakespeare placed there for his actors. With the texts side by side, you can see where and why editors have made changes and what may have been lost in translation.

In addition to being divided into Histories, Comedies, and Tragedies, the original series further breaks down speeches by the character's designated gender, also indicating speeches appropriate for any gender. Drawing from this example, this series breaks down each original volume into four workbooks: speeches for Women of all ages, Younger Men, Older Men and Any Gender. Gender is naturally fluid for Shakespeare's characters since during his time, ALL of the characters were portrayed by males. Contemporary productions of Shakespeare commonly switch character genders (Prospero has become Prospera), in addition to presenting single gender, reverse gender and gender non-specific productions. There are certainly characters and speeches where the gender is immaterial, hence the inclusion of a volume of speeches for Any Gender. This was something that Neil had indicated in the original volumes; we are merely following his example.

Once More Unto the Speech Dear Friends was a culmination of Neil's dedicated efforts to make the First Folio more accessible and available to readers and to illuminate for actors the many clues within the Folio text, as originally published. The material in this book is drawn from that work and retains Neil's British spelling of words (i.e. capitalisation) and his extensive commentary on each speech. Neil went on to continue this work as a master teacher of Shakespeare with another series of Shakespeare editions, his 'rhythm texts' and the ebook that he published on Apple Books, *The Shakespeare Variations*.

Neil published on his own First Folio editions of the plays in modern type which were the basis the Folio Texts series published by Applause of all 36 plays in the First Folio. These individual editions all have extensive notes on the changes that modern editions had made. This material was then combined to create a complete reproduction of the First Folio in modern type, *The Applause First Folio of Shakespeare in Modern Type*. These editions make the First Folio more accessible than ever before. The examples in this book demonstrate how the clues from the First Folio will give insights to understanding and performing these speeches and why it is a worthwhile endeavour to discover the riches in the First Folio.

PREFACE AND BRIEF BACKGROUND TO THE FIRST FOLIO

WHY ANOTHER SERIES OF SOLILOQUY BOOKS?

There has been an enormous change in theatre organisation recent in the last twenty years. While the major large-scale companies have continued to flourish, many small theatre companies have come into being, leading to

- much doubling
- cross gender casting, with many one time male roles now being played legitimately by/as women in updated time-period productions
- young actors being asked to play leading roles at far earlier points in their careers

All this has meant actors should be able to demonstrate enormous flexibility rather than one limited range/style. In turn, this has meant

- a change in audition expectations
- actors are often expected to show more range than ever before
- often several shorter audition speeches are asked for instead of one or two longer ones
- sometimes the initial auditions are conducted in a shorter amount of time

Thus, to stay at the top of the game, the actor needs more knowledge of what makes the play tick, especially since

- early plays demand a different style from the later ones
- the four genres (comedy, history, tragedy, and the peculiar romances) all have different acting/textual requirements
- parts originally written for the older, more experienced actors again require a different approach from those written for the younger

ones, as the young roles, especially the female ones, were played by young actors extraordinarily skilled in the arts of rhetoric

There's now much more knowledge of how the original quarto and folio texts can add to the rehearsal exploration/acting and directing process as well as to the final performance.

Each speech is made up of four parts

- a background to the speech, placing it in the context of the play, and offering line length and an approximate timing to help you choose what might be right for any auditioning occasion
- a modern text version of the speech, with the sentence structure clearly delineated side by side with
- a folio version of the speech, where modern texts changes to the capitalization, spelling and sentence structure can be plainly seen
- a commentary explaining the differences between the two texts, and in what way the original setting can offer you more information to explore

Thus if they wish, **beginners** can explore just the background and the modern text version of the speech.

An actor experienced in exploring the Folio can make use of the background and the Folio version of the speech

And those wanting to know as many details as possible and how they could help define the deft stepping stones of the arc of the speech can use all four elements on the page.

The First Folio

(FOR LIST OF CURRENT REPRODUCTIONS SEE BIBLIOGRAPHY

The end of 1623 saw the publication of the justifiably famed First Folio (F1). The single volume, published in a run of approximately 1,000 copies at the princely sum of one pound (a tremendous risk, considering that a single play would sell at no more than six pence, one fortieth of F1's price, and that the annual salary of a schoolmaster was only ten pounds), contained thirty-six plays.

The manuscripts from which each F1 play would be printed came from a variety of sources. Some had already been printed. Some came from the playhouse complete with production details. Some had no theatrical input at all, but were handsomely copied out and easy to read. Some were supposedly very messy, complete with first draft scribbles and crossings out. Yet, as Charlton Hinman, the revered dean of First Folio studies describes F1 in the Introduction to the Norton Facsimile:

> It is of inestimable value for what it is, for what it contains. For here are preserved the masterworks of the man universally recognized as our greatest writer; and preserved, as Ben Jonson realized at the time of the original publication, not for an age but for all time.

WHAT DOES F1 REPRESENT?

- texts prepared for actors who rehearsed three days for a new play and one day for one already in the repertoire
- written in a style (rhetoric incorporating debate) so different from ours (grammatical) that many modern alterations based on grammar (or poetry) have done remarkable harm to the rhetorical/debate quality of the original text and thus to interpretations of characters at key moments of stress.
- written for an acting company the core of which steadily grew older, and whose skills and interests changed markedly over twenty years as well as for an audience whose make-up and interests likewise changed as the company grew more experienced

The whole is based upon supposedly the best documents available at the time, collected by men closest to Shakespeare throughout his career, and brought to a single printing house whose errors are now widely understood - far more than those of some of the printing houses that produced the original quartos.

TEXTUAL SOURCES FOR THE AUDITION SPEECHES

Individual modern editions consulted in the preparation of the Modern Text version of the speeches are listed in the Bibliography under the separate headings 'The Complete Works in Compendium Format' and ' The Complete Works in Separate Individual Volumes.' Most of the modern versions of the speeches are a compilation of several of these texts. However, all modern act, scene and/or line numbers refer the reader to The Riverside Shakespeare, in my opinion still the best of the complete works despite the excellent compendiums that have been published since.

The First Folio versions of the speeches are taken from a variety of already published sources, including not only all the texts listed in the 'Photostatted Reproductions in Compendium Format' section of the Bibliography, but also earlier, individually printed volumes, such as the twentieth century editions published under the collective title *The Facsimiles of Plays from The First Folio of Shakespeare* by Faber & Gwyer, and the nineteenth century editions published on behalf of The New Shakespeare Society.

INTRODUCTION

So, congratulations , you've got an audition, and for a Shakespeare play no less.

You've done all your homework, including, hopefully , reading the whole play to see the full range and development of the character.

You've got an idea of the character, the situation in which you/it finds itself (the given circumstance s); what your/its needs are (objectives/ intentions); and what you intend to do about them (action /tactics).

You've looked up all the unusual words in a good dictionary or glossary; you've turned to a well edited modern edition to find out what some of the more obscure references mean.

And those of you who understand metre and rhythm have worked on the poetic values of the speech, and you are word perfect . . .

. . . and yet it's still not working properly and/or you feel there's more to be gleaned from the text , but you're not sure what that something is or how to go about getting at it; in other words, all is not quite right, yet.

THE KEY QUESTION
What text have you been working with - a good modern text or an 'original' text, that is a copy of one of the first printings of the play?

If it's a modern text, no matter how well edited (and there are some splendid single copy editions available, see the Bibliography for further details), despite all the learned information offered, it's not surprising you feel somewhat at a loss, for there is a huge difference between the original printings (the First Folio, and the individual quartos, see

Appendix 1 for further details) and any text prepared after 1700 right up to the most modern of editions. All the post 1700 texts have been tidied-up for the modern reader to ingest silently, revamped according to the rules of correct grammar, syntax and poetry. However the 'originals' were prepared for actors speaking aloud playing characters often in a great deal of emotional and/or intellectual stress, and were set down on paper according to the very flexible rules of rhetoric and a seemingly very cavalier attitude towards the rules of grammar, and syntax, and spelling, and capitalisation, and even poetry.

Unfortunately, because of the grammatical and syntactical standardisation in place by the early 1700's, many of the quirks and oddities of the origin also have been dismissed as 'accidental' - usually as compositor error either in deciphering the original manuscript, falling prey to their own particular idosyncracies, or not having calculated correctly the amount of space needed to set the text. Modern texts dismiss the possibility that these very quirks and oddities may be by Shakespeare, hearing his characters in as much difficulty as poor Peter Quince is in *A Midsummer Night's Dream* (when he, as the Prologue, terrified and struck down by stage fright, makes a huge grammatical hash in introducing his play 'Pyramus and Thisbe' before the aristocracy, whose acceptance or otherwise, can make or break him)

> If we offend, it is with our good will.
> That you should think, we come not to offend,
> But with good will.
>   To show our simple skill,
> That is the true beginning of our end .
> Consider then, we come but in despite.
> We do not come, as minding to content you ,
> Our true intent is.
>   All for your delight
> We are not here.
>   That you should here repent you,

The Actors are at hand; and by their show,
You shall know all, that you are like to know.

(A *Midsummer Night's Dream*)

In many other cases in the complete works what was originally printed is equally 'peculiar,' but, unlike Peter Quince , these peculiarities are usually regularised by most modern texts.

However, this series of volumes is based on the belief - as the following will show - that most of these 'peculiarities' resulted from Shakespeare setting down for his actors the stresses, trials, and tribulations the characters are experiencing as they think and speak, and thus are theatrical gold-dust for the actor, director, scholar, teacher, and general reader alike.

THE FIRST ESSENTIAL DIFFERENCE BETWEEN THE TWO TEXTS

THINKING

A **modern** text can show
- the story line
- your character's conflict with the world at large
- your character's conflict with certain individuals within that world

but because of the very way an 'original' text was set, it can show you all this plus one key extra, the very thing that makes big speeches what they are

- the conflict within the character

WHY?

Any good playwright writes about characters in stressful situations who are often in a state of conflict not only with the world around them and the people in that world, but also within themselves. And you probably know from personal experience that when these conflicts occur peo-

Neil Freeman   21

ple do not necessarily utter the most perfect of grammatical/poetic/ syntactic statements, phrases, or sentences. Joy and delight, pain and sorrow often come sweeping through in the way things are said, in the incoherence of the phrases, the running together of normally disassociated ideas, and even in the sounds of the words themselves.

The tremendous advantage of the period in which Shakespeare was setting his plays down on paper and how they first appeared in print was that when characters were rational and in control of self and situation, their phrasing and sentences (and poetic structure) would appear to be quite normal even to a modern eye - but when things were going wrong, so sentences and phrasing (and poetic structure) would become highly erratic. But the Quince type eccentricities are rarely allowed to stand. Sadly, in tidying, most modern texts usually make the text far too clean, thus setting rationality when none originally existed.

THE SECOND ESSENTIAL DIFFERENCE BETWEEN THE TWO TEXTS
SPEAKING, ARGUING, DEBATING

Having discovered what and how you/your character is thinking is only the first stage of the work - you/it then have to speak aloud, in a society that absolutely loved to speak - and not only speak ideas (content) but to speak entertainingly so as to keep listeners enthralled (and this was especially so when you have little content to offer and have to mask it somehow - think of today's television adverts and political spin doctors as a parallel and you get the picture). Indeed one of the Elizabethan 'how to win an argument' books was very precise about this - George Puttenham, *The Art of English Poesie* (1589).

A: ELIZABETHAN SCHOOLING

All educated classes could debate/argue at the drop of a hat, for both boys (in 'petty-schools') and girls (by books and tutors) were trained in what was known overall as the art of rhetoric, which itself was split into three parts

- first, how to distinguish the real from false appearances/outward show (think of the three caskets in *The Merchant of Venice* where the language on the gold and silver caskets enticingly, and deceptively, seems to offer hopes of great personal rewards that are dashed when the language is carefully explored, whereas once the apparent threat on the lead casket is carefully analysed the reward therein is the greatest that could be hoped for)
- second, how to frame your argument on one of 'three great grounds'; honour/morality; justice/legality; and, when all else fails, expedience/ practicality.
- third, how to order and phrase your argument so winsomely that your audience will vote for you no matter how good the opposition - and there were well over two hundred rules and variations by which winning could be achieved, all of which had to be assimilated before a child's education was considered over and done with.

B: THINKING ON YOUR FEET: I.E. THE QUICK, DEFT , RAPID MODIFICATION OF EACH TINY THOUGHT

The Elizabethan/therefore your character/therefore you were also trained to explore and modify your thoughts as you spoke - never would you see a sentence in its entirety and have it perfectly worked out in your mind before you spoke (unless it was a deliberately written, formal public declaration, as with the Officer of the Court in The Winter' s Tale, reading the charges against Hermione). Thus after uttering your very first phrase, you might expand it, or modify it, deny it, change it, and so on throughout the whole sentence and speech.

From the poet Samuel Coleridge Taylor there is a wonderful description of how Shakespeare puts thoughts together like "a serpent twisting and untwisting in its own strength," that is, with one thought springing out of the one previous. Treat each new phrase as a fresh unravelling of the serpent's coil. What is discovered (and therefore said) is only revealed as the old coil/phrase disappears revealing a new coil in its place. The new coil is the new thought. The old coil moves/disappears because the previous phrase is finished with as soon as it is spoken.

C: MODERN APPLICATION

It is very rarely we speak dispassionately in our 'real' lives, after all thoughts give rise to feelings, feelings give rise to thoughts, and we usually speak both together - unless

1/ we're trying very hard for some reason to control ourselves and not give ourselves away

2/ or the volcano of emotions within us is so strong that we cannot control ourselves, and feelings swamp thoughts

3/ and sometimes whether deliberately or unconsciously we colour words according to our feelings; the humanity behind the words so revealed is instantly understandable.

D: HOW THE ORIGINAL TEXTS NATURALLY ENHANCE/ UNDERSCORE THIS CONTROL OR RELEASE

The amazing thing about the way all Elizabethan/early Jacobean texts were first set down (the term used to describe the printed words on the page being 'orthography'), is that it was flexible, it allowed for such variations to be automatically set down without fear of grammatical repercussion.

So if Shakespeare heard Juliet's nurse working hard to try to convince Juliet that the Prince's nephew Juliet is being forced to (bigamously) marry, instead of setting the everyday normal

'O he's a lovely gentleman'

which the modern texts HAVE to set, the first printings were permitted to set

'O hee's a Lovely Gentleman'

suggesting that something might be going on inside the Nurse that causes her to release such excessive extra energy.

E: BE CAREFUL

This needs to be stressed very carefully: the orthography doesn't dictate to you/force you to accept exactly what it means. The orthography simply suggests you might want to explore this moment further or more deeply.

In other words, simply because of the flexibility with which the Elizabethans/Shakespeare could set down on paper what they heard in their minds or wanted their listeners to hear, in addition to all the modern acting necessities of character - situation, objective, intention, action, and tactics the original Shakespeare texts offer pointers to where feelings (either emotional or intellectual, or when combined together as passion, both) are also evident.

SUMMARY

BASIC APPROACH TO THE SPEECHES SHOWN BELOW

(after reading the 'background')

1/ first use the modern version shown in the first column: by doing so you can discover

- the basic plot line of what's happening to the character, and
- the first set of conflicts/obstacles impinging on the character as a result of the situation or actions of other characters
- the supposed grammatical and poetical correctnesses of the speech

2/ then you can explore

- any acting techniques you'd apply to any modern soliloquy, including establishing for the character
- the given circumstances of the scene
- their outward state of being (who they are sociologically, etc.)
- their intentions and objectives
- the resultant action and tactics they decide to pursue

3/ when this is complete, turn to the First Folio version of the text, shown on the facing page: this will help you discover and explore

- the precise thinking and debating process so essential to an understanding of any Shakespeare text
- the moments when the text is NOT grammatically or poetically as correct as the modern texts would have you believe, which will in turn help you recognise
- the moments of conflict and struggle stemming from within the character itself
- the sense of fun and enjoyment the Shakespeare language nearly always offers you no matter how dire the situation

4/ should you wish to further explore even more the differences between the two texts, the commentary that follows discusses how the First Folio has been changed, and what those alterations might mean for the human arc of the speech

NOTES ON HOW THESE SPEECHES ARE SET UP

For each of the speeches the first page will include the Background on the speech and other information including number of lines, approximate timing and who is addressed. Then will follow a spread which shows the modern text version on the left and the First Folio version on the right, followed by a page of Commentary.

PROBABLE TIMING: (shown on the Background page before the speeches begin, set below the number of lines) 0.45 = a forty-five second speech

SYMBOLS & ABBREVIATIONS IN THE COMMENTARY AND TEXT

F: the First Folio

mt.: modern texts

F # followed by a number: the number of the sentence under discussion in the First Folio version of the speech, thus F #7 would refer to the seventh sentence

mt. # followed by a numb er: the number of the sentence under discussion in the modern text version of the speech, thus mt. #5 would refer to the fifth sentence

 # /#, (e.g. 3/7): the first number refers to the number of capital letters in the passage under discussion; the second refers to the number of long spellings therein

within a quotation from the speech: / indicates where one verse line ends and a fresh one starts

[ ] : set around words in both texts when F1 sets one word , mt another

{ } : some minor alteration has been made, in a speech built up, where, a word or phrase will be changed, added, or removed

{†} : this symbol shows where a sizeable part of the text is omitted

TERMS FOUND IN THE COMMENTARY
OVERALL

1/ **orthography**: the capitalization, spellings, punctuation of the First Folio

SIGNS OF IMPORTANT DISCOVERIES/ARGUMENTS WITHIN A FIRST FOLIO SPEECH

2/ **major punctuation**: colons and semicolons: since the Shakespeare texts are based so much on the art of debate and argument, the importance of F1's major punctuation must not be underestimated, for both the semicolon (;) and colon (:) mark a moment of importance for the character, either for itself, as a moment of discovery or revelation, or as a key point in a discussion, argument or debate that it wishes to impress upon other characters onstage

as a rule of thumb:

a/ the more frequent colon (:) suggests that whatever the power of the point discovered or argued, the character is not side-tracked and can continue with the argument - as such, the colon can be regarded as a **logical** connection

b/ the far less frequent semicolon (;) suggests that because of the power inherent in the point discovered or argued, the character is side-tracked and momentarily loses the argument and falls back into itself or can only continue the argument with great difficulty - as such, the semicolon should be regarded as an **emotional** connection

3/ **surround phrases**: phrase(s) surrounded by major punctuation, or a combination of major punctuation and the end or beginning of a sentence: thus these phrases seem to be of especial importance for both character and speech, well worth exploring as key to the argument made and /or emotions released

DIALOGUE NOT FOUND IN THE FIRST FOLIO
∞ set where modern texts add dialogue from a quarto text which has not been included in F1

A LOOSE RULE OF THUMB TO THE THINKING PROCESS OF A FIRST FOLIO CHARACTER

1/ mental discipline/**intellect**: a section where capitals dominate suggests that the intellectual reason ing behind what is being spoken or discovered is of more concern than the personal response beneath it

2/ feelings/**emotions**: a section where long spellings dominate suggests that the personal response to what is being spoken or discovered is of more concern than the intellectual reasoning behind it

3/ **passion**: a section where both long spellings and capitals are present in almost equal proportions suggests that both mind and emotion/feelings are inseparable, and thus the character is speaking passionately

SIGNS OF LESS THAN GRAMMATICAL THINKING WITHIN A FIRST FOLIO SPEECH

1/ **onrush**: sometimes thoughts are coming so fast that several topics are joined together as one long sentence suggesting that the F character's mind is working very quickly, or that his/her emotional state is causing some concern: most mod ern texts split such a sentence into several grammatically correct parts (the opening speech of *As You Like It* is a fine example, where F's long 18 line opening sentence is split into six): while the modern texts' resetting may be syntactically correct, the F moment is nowhere near as calm as the revisions suggest

2/ **fast-link**: sometimes F shows thoughts moving so quickly for a character that the connecting punctuation between disparate topics is merely a comma, suggesting that there is virtually no pause in springing from one idea to the next: unfortunately most modern texts rarely allow this to stand, instead replacing the obviously disturbed comma with a grammatical period, once more creating calm that it seems the original texts never intended to show

FIRST FOLIO SIGNS OF WHEN VERBAL GAME PLAYING HAS TO STOP

1/ **non-embellished:** a section with neither capitals nor long spellings suggests that what is being discovered or spoken is so important to the character that there is no time to guss it up with vocal or mental excesses: an unusual moment of self-control

2/ **short sentence:** coming out of a society where debate was second nature, man y of Shakespeare's characters speak in long sentences in which ideas are stated, explored, redefined and summarized all before moving onto the next idea in the argument, discovery or debate: the longer sentence is the sign of a rhetorically trained mind used to public speaking (oratory), but at times an idea or discovery is so startling or inevitable that length is either unnecessary or impossible to maintain : hence the occasional very important short sentence suggests that there is no time for the niceties of oratorical adornment with which to sugar the pill - verbal games are at an end and now the basic core of the issue must be faced

3/ **monosyllabic:** with English being composed of two strands, the polysyllabic (stemming from French, Italian, Latin and Greek), and the monosyllabic (from the Anglo-Saxon), each strand has two distinct functions: the polysyllabic words are often used when there is time for fanciful elaboration and rich description (which could be described as 'excessive rhetoric') while the monosyllabic occur when, literally, there is no other way of putting a basic question or comment - Juliet's "Do you love me? I know thou wilt say aye" is a classic example of both monosyllables and non-embellishment: with monosyllables, only the naked truth is being spoken, nothing is hidden

Monologues from Shakespeare's First Folio for Women:
The Tragedies

The Lamentable Tragedie of Titus Andronicus

Tamora

Stay Romaine Bretheren, gracious Conqueror,
1.1.104 - 120

Background: to offset the death of his two sons in the recent conflict, the Roman Titus is preparing to sacrifice the Goth Tamora's eldest son Alarbus; in the following, Tamora pleads, unsuccessfully, for her son's life to be spared

Style: public address in the open air on behalf of all present

Where: unspecified, but a public square in Rome

To Whom: Titus, in front of a large group, comprised of his four sons, daughter Lavinia and brother Marcus; Tamora and her three sons; the emperor's two sons and their followers; Tribunes and Senators

# of Lines: 17

Probable Timing: 0.55 minutes

Take Note: Modern texts alter F's sentence structure on three occasions, and in so doing create a far more melodramatic yet rational character than originally set. F's structure and orthography establish the more human dynamics of a high-status mother in pain.

Tamora

1　Stay, Roman brethren!

2　Gracious conqueror,
　Victorious Titus, rue the tears I shed,
　A mother's tears in passion for her son;
　And if thy sons were ever dear to thee,
　O think my sons to be as dear to me!

3　Sufficeth not that we are brought to Rome
　To beautify thy triumphs, and return
　Captive to thee, and to thy Roman yoke;
　But must my sons be slaughtered in the streets
　For valiant doings in their country's cause?

4　O, if to fight for king and commonweal
　Were piety in thine, it is in these.

5　Andronicus, stain not thy tomb with blood!

6　Wilt thou draw near the nature of the gods?

7　Draw near them then in being merciful:
　Sweet mercy is nobility's true badge.

8　Thrice-noble Titus, spare my first-born son!

Tamora

1　Stay Romaine Bretheren, gracious Conqueror,
　Victorious Titus, rue the teares I shed,
　A Mothers teares in passion for her sonne :
　And if thy Sonnes were ever deere to thee,
　Oh thinke my sonnes to be as deere to mee.

2　Sufficeth not, that we are brought to Rome
　To beautifie thy Triumphs, and returne
　Captive to thee, and to thy Romaine yoake,
　But must my Sonnes be slaughtred in the streetes,
　For Valiant doings in their Countries cause?

3　O!

4　　　If to fight for King and Common-weale,
　Were piety in thine, it is in these :
　Andronicus, staine not thy Tombe with blood.

5　Wilt thou draw neere the nature of the Gods?

6　Draw neere them then in being mercifull.

7　Sweet mercy is Nobilities true badge,
　Thrice Noble Titus, spare my first borne sonne.

- Tamora's F opening plea is far more speedy and direct without the extra comma and exclamation mark modern texts add to the first line, especially when coupled with F's setting of the opening as one emotional sentence instead of modern texts' more rational two

- the mental and emotional struggle battling within her is clearly marked in three separate stages in the opening F sentence

  a/ line 1 is essentially debate and public speech oriented (3/1), presumably to grab everyone's attention

  b/ in the next two lines (speaking as a mother) feeling begins to swamp the intellect (2/3)

  c/ and emotion floods the two remaining lines of F #1 (1/6)

- and this struggle is seen again in the final F sentence, with the appeal inherent in the first line and half intellectually driven ('Nobilitie', 'Noble Titus' - 3/0) only to finish emotionally once more (0/2 in the last phrase) as she pleads for her 'first borne sonne'

- her F struggle is more marked, for this last F sentence's somewhat ungrammatical blurt is split into a more controlled and rhetorical two sentence appeal in modern texts

- the single surround phrase " : Andronicus, staine not thy Tombe with blood . " is, whether consciously or not, remarkably prescient as regards the remaining action of the play, foreshadowing both her desire for revenge and the tragedies that befall the house of Andronicus

The Lamentable Tragedie of Titus Andronicus

Tamora

Have I not reason thinke you to looke pale.

2.3.91 - 115

Background: though now empress of Rome, Tamora has maintained a
lover from days as Queene of the Goths, Aaron the Moore: they have
been discovered in a compromising situation by two of her perceived
enemies, Titus' daughter Lavinia and her husband Bassianus, younger brother to Tamora's new husband, Saturninus: they threaten to
tell Saturninus, fortunately for Tamora, but not Lavinia or Bassianus,
Tamora's sons Chiron and Demetrius appear, to whom she immediately tells the following lies (which eventually results in her sons
killing Bassianus, and raping and mutilating Lavinia)

Style: as part of a six handed scene

Where: in the woods

To Whom: in front of her lover Aaron, her sons Chiron and Demetrius,
and Lavinia and Bassianus

# of Lines: 25

Probable Timing: 1.15 minutes

Take Note: Yet again modern texts alter F's Tamora's sentence structure.
While it may be logical to rework the end of F's sentence #2 into a
larger whole (mt. #2) this interferes with her overworked attempts at
scene setting the supposed horror of the event.

Tamora

1　Have I not reason, think you, to look pale ?

2　These two have tic'd me hither to this place :
　A barren, detested vale you see it is;
　The trees, though summer, yet forlorn and lean,
　[Overcome] with moss and baleful mistletoe;
　Here never shines the sun, here nothing breeds,
　Unless the nightly owl, or fatal raven ;
　And when they show'd me this abhorred pit,
　They told me, here, at dead time of the night,
　A thousand fiends, a thousand hissing snakes,
　Ten thousand swelling toads, as many urchins,
　Would make such fearful and confused cries,
　As any mortal body hearing it
　Should straight fall mad, or else die suddenly.

3　No sooner had they told this hellish tale,
　But straight they told me they would bind me here
　Unto the body of a dismal yew,
　And leave me to this miserable death !

4　And then they call'd me foul adulteress,
　Lascivious Goth, and all the bitterest terms
　That ever ear did hear to such effect;
　And had you not by wondrous fortune come,
　This vengeance on me had they executed :
　Revenge it, as you love your mother's life,
　Or be ye not henceforth call'd my children.

Tamora

1   Have I not reason thinke you to looke pale.

2   These two have tic'd me hither to this place,
    A barren, detested vale you see it is.

3   The Trees though Sommer, yet forlorne and leane,
    [Ore-come] with Mosse, and balefull Misselto.

4   Heere never shines the Sunne, heere nothing breeds,
    Unlesse the nightly Owle, or fatall Raven :
    And when they shew'd me this abhorred pit,
    They told me heere at dead time of the night,
    A thousand Fiends, a thousand hissing Snakes,
    Ten thousand swelling Toades, as many Urchins,
    Would make such fearefull and confused cries,
    As any mortall body hearing it,
    Should straite fall mad, or else die suddenly.

5   No sooner had they told this hellish tale,
    But strait they told me they would binde me heere,
    Unto the body of a dismall yew,
    And leave me to this miserable death.

6   And then they call'd me foule Adulteresse,
    Lascivious Goth, and all the bitterest tearmes
    That ever eare did heare to such effect.

7   And had you not by wondrous fortune come,
    This vengeance on me had they executed :
    Revenge it, as you love your Mothers life,
    Or be ye not henceforth cal'd my Children.

While resetting the two sentences ending the F text may be grammatically understandable, it reduces the extra (again perhaps fake) melodramatic oomph she has in the final F appeal for revenge, especially when the subtle variations in the orthography of F's #6 and #7 are added to the mix.

• unusually for Tamora, especially at supposedly crucial moments, here there are times where there is no embellishment, as if it takes her an effort just to tell her tale viz.

"These two have tic'd me hither to this place,
A barren, detested vale you see it is ."
"And when they shew'd me this abhorred pit,"
"No sooner had they told this hellish tale,"
"And leave me to this miserable death ."
"And had you not by wondrous fortune come,
This vengeance on me had they executed :"

(again, perhaps the sign of a superb villainess acting out her role)

• that there are more long spellings to capitals is only to be expected (25/15), but its interesting to see how the capitals fall into place in two major sets, as with the supposedly (at least to most women) frightening images of sentences F #3-4 (11 of the 15), and then appeal to family loyalty in the last two lines of the speech, once she says she has been called 'Adultresse', and 'lascivious Goth'

• and with the sea of long spellings (2 in the first line; 4 in just two lines of F #3; 6 in the first two lines of F #4; 5 in the three lines of F #6) it's fascinating to see there are none in her last F sentence, as she moves her sons to 'vengeance' (almost as if the game playing were now complete and no longer necessary)

The Tragedie of
Romeo and Juliet

Juliet

Thou knowest the maske of night is on my face,
2.2.85 - 106

Background: having heard Juliet's closest secrets Romeo has sprung
from his hiding place declaring his love, initially giving Juliet a
great shock, since initially she can't see him and has no idea who is
being so passionate: once she discovers who it is, and that he is here
because it is 'Love that first did promp me to enquire', she unequiv-
ocally confesses her (somewhat mixed) feelings

Style: as part of a two-handed scene

Where: on her balcony

To Whom: Romeo, below

# of Lines: 22

Probable Timing: 1.10 minutes

Take Note: Unlike the previous passionate speech (13/10 overall)
when Juliet was alone and emotions rarely took over, now she is
with Romeo though the speech again seems overall passionate
(11/15) her emotions almost swamp her, at least as the speech starts.

Juliet

1   Thou knowest the mask of night is on my face,
    Else would a maiden blush bepaint my cheek
    For that which thou hast heard me speak to-night.

2   Fain would I dwell on form, fain, fain deny
    What I have spoke, but farewell compliment!

3   Dost thou love [me]?

4   I know thou wilt say, ["Ay"],
    And I will take thy word; yet, if thou swear'st,
    Thou mayest prove false: at lovers' perjuries
    They say Jove [laughs].

5   O gentle Romeo,
    If thou dost love, pronounce it faithfully;
    Or if thou thinkest I am too quickly won,
    I'll frown and be perverse, and say thee nay,
    So thou wilt woo, but else not for the world.

6   In truth, fair [Montague], I am too fond:
    And therefore thou mayest think my [havior] light,
    But trust me, gentleman, I'll prove more true,
    [Than] those that have [more cunning] to be strange.

7   I should have been more strange, I must confess,
    But that thou over heard'st, ere I was ware,
    My true-[love] passion; therefore pardon me,
    And not impute this yielding to light love,
    Which the dark night hath so discovered.

Juliet

1   Thou knowest the maske of night is on my face,
Else would a Maiden blush bepaint my cheeke,
For that which thou hast heard me speake to night,
Faine would I dwell on forme, faine, faine, denie
What I have spoke, but farewell Complement,
Doest thou Love [ ] ?

2   I know thou wilt say [I],
And I will take thy word, yet if thou swear'st,
Thou maiest prove false : at Lovers perjuries
They say Jove [laught], oh gentle Romeo,
If thou dost Love, pronounce it faithfully :
Or if thou thinkest I am too quickly wonne,
Ile frowne and be perverse, and say thee nay,
So thou wilt wooe : But else not for the world.

3   In truth faire [Mountague] I am too fond :
And therefore thou maiest thinke my [behaviour] light,
But trust me Gentleman, Ile prove more true,
[Then] those that have [coying] to be strange,
I should have beene more strange, I must confesse,
But that thou over heard'st ere I was ware
My true [Loves] passion, therefore pardon me,
And not impute this yeelding to light Love,
Which the darke night hath so discovered.

- hardly surprisingly, Juliet's initial confession starts emotionally (1/7, F #4's first four lines), but an intellectual determination to speak her mind floods F #1's last line (2/0)

- following her F #2's unembellished opening fears that Romeo 'maiest prove false', her explanation that 'Jove laught' at 'Lovers perjuries' is intellectual (4/1, the two and a half lines between F #2's first two colons), while the suggestion she would play the courting game of nay-saying if it would better his opinion of her becomes emotional once more (1/3, F #3's last three lines save for the final unembellished phrase)

- F#3's confession of being 'too fond' becomes very subdued, with only three releases in the first six lines, while the denial that hers is a 'light Love' becomes adamantly passionate (2/2 in the last three lines)

- the few unembellished passages very clearly, carefully, and vulnerably point to her concerns: first as to her fears about possible betrayal (opening F #2), heightened further by being monosyllabic

  "I know thou wilt say I,/And I will take thy word, yet if thou swear'st, /Thou maiest prove false :"

  and then the occasional unembellished phrases referring to the depth of her own love are equally telling 'I am too fond'; 'Ile prove more true'; 'I should have beene more strange . . . /But that thou over heard'st ere I was ware'; and 'therefore pardon me'

- and the two surround phrases also point to the strength of her love, the end of F #2 emphasising she doesn't want to play courting denial games

  " : But else not for the world . "

  and the opening of F #3

  " . In truth faire Mountague I am too fond : "

The Tragedie of
Romeo and Juliet

Juliet

The clocke strook nine, when I did send the Nurse,
2.5.1 - 19

Background: Juliet is waiting for the nurse to return from her meeting with Romeo: unfortunately, though the Nurse left at nine, she didn't meet Romeo until, as Mercutio brazenly put it, 'when the bawdy hand of the Dyall' was 'upon the pricke of noone', so she is very, very late

Style: solo

Where: presumably outside in the grounds of the Capulet residence

To Whom: self, and direct audience address

# of Lines: 19

Probable Timing: 1.00 minutes

Take Note: Since she has been waiting three hours for the Nurse's return (which was scheduled for two and half hours ago) the fact that the first three lines are highly emotional (1/6) and end in a surround phrase pushing aside thoughts of doom (' : that's not so : ') is hardly surprising.

Background

Juliet

1 The clock struck nine, when I did send the Nurse ;
   In half an hour she promised to return.

2 Perchance she cannot meet him - that's not so .

3 O, she is lame !

4 Love's [heralds] should be thoughts,
   Which ten times faster glides [than] the sun's beams,
   Driving back shadows over low'ring hills;
   Therefore do nimble-pinion'd doves draw Love,
   And therefore hath the wind-swift Cupid wings .

5 Now is the sun upon the highmost hill
   Of this day's journey, and from nine till twelve
   [Is] three long hours, yet she is not come .

6 Had she affections and warm youthful blood,
   She would be as swift in motion as a ball ;
   My words would bandy her to my sweet love,
   And his to me .

7 But old folks - many feign as they were dead,
   Unwieldy, slow, heavy, and pale as lead .

Enter Nurse

8 O God, she comes !

9 O honey nurse what news?

10 Hast thou met with him ?

11 Send thy man away.

Juliet

1   The clocke strook nine, when I did send the Nurse,
    In halfe an houre she promised to returne,
    Perchance she cannot meete him : that's not so :
    Oh she is lame, Loves [Herauld] should be thoughts,
    Which ten times faster glides [then] the Sunnes beames,
    Driving backe shadowes over lowring hils.

2   Therefore do nimble Pinion'd Doves draw Love,
    And therefore hath the wind-swift Cupid wings :
    Now is the Sun upon the highmost hill
    Of this daies journey, and from nine till twelve,
    [I] three long houres, yet she is not come.

3   Had she affections and warme youthfull blood,
    She would be as swift in motion as a ball,
    My words would bandy her to my sweete Love,
    And his to me, but old folkes,
    Many faine as they were dead,
    Unwieldie, slow, heavy, and pale as lead.

                    Enter Nurse

4   O God she comes, O hony Nurse what newes?

5   Hast thou met with him? send thy man away.

- the attempt to justify the Nurse's lateness ('Oh she is lame, . . .') at least adds some intellectual control to the speech (3/6)

- which gains more headway as she dwells on classical love images (4/0, F #2's first two lines), but the untroubled mood doesn't seem to last

- for F #2's last three lines, ending with the monosyllabic unembellished 'yet she is not come', becomes much less exuberant (1/1)

- and this quietness (an attempt not to give in to emotion? or a quiet pout perhaps?) continues through the mildly emotional F #3 denigration of 'old folkes' (1/3 in six lines)

- however, the enormity of her images' attack are underscored both by

  a/ the pauses inherent before voicing the melodramatic exaggeration contained in the two unusual short lines 'And his to me, but old folkes,/Many faine as they were dead' (7/7 syllables, the impact reduced by most modern texts resetting the passage as just one short line followed by one of regular length 4/10 syllables)

  b/ and the two unembellished lines that if the Nurse were young and had 'affections', 'She would be as swift in motion as a ball,' and the less than flattering description as Juliet finds her to be 'Unwieldie, slow, heavy and pale as lead.'

- yet when the Nurse enters all control momentarily disappears with F #4's excited intellect of 'O God she comes, . . .' (3/0), only to be followed by F #5's two short unembellished surround phrases that end the speech

The Tragedie of
Romeo and Juliet

Juliet

What storme is this that blowes so contrarie?
between 3.2.64 - 85

Background: in her grief, for Tybalt was 'the best Friend' she had, the Nurse has not made it clear who is dead: as a result Juliet has believed that it was Romeo who has died, until the Nurse's comment 'O Tybalt . . . /That ever I should live to see thee dead' triggers the following

Style: as part of a two-handed scene

Where: either in Juliet's chambers or the grounds of the Capulet's residence

To Whom: the Nurse

# of Lines: 17

Probable Timing: 0.55 minutes

Take Note: Given the appalling news of Tybalt's death at the hands of her new husband Romeo, and of Romeo's banishment, it is hardly surprising F's orthography shows little or no consistency from one moment to the next.

Juliet

1   What storm is this that blows so contrary?

2   Did Romeo's hand shed Tybalt's blood?
     It did, it did, alas the day, it did.

3/{†}O serpent heart, hid with a flow'ring face!

4   Did ever dragon keep so fair a cave?

5   Beautiful tyrant! fiend angelical!
     [ ] Dove-feather'd raven, wolvish-ravening lamb!
     Despised substance of divinest show!
     Just opposite to what thou justly seem'st,
     A [damned] saint, an honorable villain!

6   O nature! what had'st thou to do in hell
     When thou did'st bower the spirit of a fiend
     In mortal paradise of such sweet flesh?

7   Was ever book containing such vile matter
     So fairly bound?

8   O that deceit should dwell
     In such a gorgeous palace!

Juliet

1   What storme is this that blowes so contrarie?

---

2   Did Rom'os hand shed Tybalts blood
     It did, it did, alas the day, it did.

3/{†}O Serpent heart, hid with a flowring face.

4   Did ever Dragon keepe so faire a Cave?

5   Beautifull Tyrant, fiend Angelicall :
     [Ravenous] Dove-feather'd Raven,
     Wolvish-ravening Lambe,
     Dispised substance of Divinest show :
     Just opposite to what thou justly seem'st,
     A [dimne] Saint, an Honourable Villaine :
     O Nature! what had'st thou to doe in hell,
     When thou did'st bower the spirit of a fiend
     In mortall paradise of such sweet flesh?
     Was ever booke containing such vile matter
     So fairely bound?

6   O that deceit should dwell
     In such a gorgeous Pallace.

- thus F #1's short immediate response is emotional (0/2), while, F #2-3's demand for confirmation is a combination of intellect (3/0) and an unembellished monosyllabic line as Juliet realises the truth 'It did, it did, alas the day, it did.'

- the list of her tormented love-hate descriptions of Romeo are deeply passionate (6/6, F #4 and the first four lines of F #5), the strain she's undergoing heightened by both F #5'sonrush, opening with a surround phrase and the needed pauses implicit in the following two short lines (five to seven/five or six syllables) - the impact of which is removed by most modern texts which combine them as one longer line

- the nakedly unembellished quiet, 'Just opposite to what thou justly seem'st' suggests she can hardly voice the fear that that she's deceived herself as to Romeo's goodness

- and as the attempt to reconcile/identify the opposites of a '[damned] Saint' and 'Honourable Villaine' pull her apart in just a line and a half as she springs back to passion (4/3)

- F #5's final four lines of berating nature becomes emotional (0/4), while the final still unresolved assessment turns slightly passionate once more (F #6. 1/1)

The Tragedie of
Romeo and Juliet
Nurse

Mistris, what Mistris? Juliet? Fast I warrant her she.
4.5.1 - 13

Background: early in the morning of the wedding to Paris, the nurse has come to ready Juliet for the ceremony, unaware of the Frier's sleep 'like Death' potion which Juliet has taken to save her from the bigamous marriage and betrayal of Romeo

Style: solo

Where: Juliet's chamber

To Whom: self, audience, and the sleeping Juliet

# of Lines: 13

Probable Timing: 0.45 minutes

Take Note: F sets no exclamation marks (!), but rather has the Nurse call to Juliet with gentle (sometimes oratorical) questions – the gentleness is hardly surprising since, thanks to the forthcoming marriage, this is presumably the last time the Nurse will be called upon to do such a task, indeed it may be the last she'll ever be alone with Juliet. Most modern texts replace at least six of the question marks and three commas with exclamation points (often setting more than thirteen of them) suggesting it is a much more robust speech than originally conceived.

Background

Nurse

1 Mistress! what mistress!

2   Juliet!

3   Fast, I warrant her, she.

4 Why, lamb! why, lady! fie, you slug-a-bed!

5 Why, love, I say! madam! sweet heart! why, bride!

6 What, not a word?

7   You take your pennyworths now;
Sleep for a week, for the next night, I warrant,
The County Paris hath set up his rest,
That you shall rest but little.

8   God forgive me!

9 Marry and amen!

10   How sound is she asleep!

11 I [needs must] wake her.

12   Madam, Madam, Madam.
[Ay], let the County take you in your bed,
He'll fright you up, ifaith.

13   Will it not be?

14 What, dress'd, and in your clothes, and down again?

15 I must needs wake you.

16   Lady, lady, lady?

Nurse

1   Mistris, what Mistris?

2   Juliet?

3   Fast I warrant her she.

4   Why Lambe, why Lady? fie you sluggabed.

5   Why Love I say?

6   Madam, sweet heart : why Bride?

7   What not a word?

8   You take your peniworths now.

9   Sleepe for a weeke, for the next night I warrant
    The Countie Paris hath set up his rest,
    That you shall rest but little, God forgive me :
    Marrie and Amen : how sound is she a sleepe?

10 I [must needs] wake her : Madam, Madam, Madam,
    [I], let the Countie take you in your bed,
    Heele fright you up yfaith.

11   Will it not be?

12 What drest, and in your clothes, and downe againe?

13 I must needs wake you : Lady, Lady, Lady?

• the speech is essentially factually/intellectually driven (17/8 overall), the few emotional moments coming in three clusters, two rather risqué jokes about love-making, 'Sleepe for a weeke', as a prelude to what Paris probably intends that night, ending with 'Heele fright you up yfaith.', and the final last two word surprise at finding Juliet already 'drest, and in your clothes, and downe againe?'

• the opening of the speech moves much faster than most modern texts suggest, for they add twelve pieces of punctuation (shown as in the F text) in the first five lines of the speech

• charmingly (or exasperatedly perhaps)the fact of Juliet staying asleep is handled via four short unembellished sentences 'Fast I warrant her she.'; 'What not a word? You take your peniworths now.'; 'Will it not be?'

The Tragedie of
Julius Cæsar
Portia

Nor for yours neither. Y'have ungently Brutus
2.1.236 - 256

Background: Already disturbed at Brutus' apparent withdrawal from
their hitherto exemplary marriage of equals, and by his sudden lack
of sleep and disinterest in food, or her, his unwell wife Portia is
further disturbed by so many men having visited him late at night,
who, despite the dark, seem to have taken great pains to muffle
themselves from public view. The following are her attempts to get
him to share with her all his thoughts as he once did - as such each
speech seems self-explanatory. This is her opening, triggered by
his attempt to side-track her with 'It is not for your health, thus to
commit/Your weake condition, to the raw cold morning'.

Style: as part of a two-handed scene

Where: in the garden of Brutus' and Portia's home

To Whom: Brutus

# of Lines: 20

Probable Timing: 1.00 minutes

Take Note: For most of the time Portia's attempt to get a response
from Brutus by simply stating the facts is handled very carefully,
as the large numbers of unembellished lines show - though, as the
speech develops, the imbalance of emotional releases quickly shows
how difficult she is finding it to maintain self-control.

Background

Portia

1　Nor for yours neither.

2　　　　　　　　　　　Y' have ungently, Brutus,
　Stole from my bed; and yesternight at supper
　You suddenly arose and walk'd about,
　Musing and sighing, with your arms across;
　And when I ask'd you what the matter was,
　You star'd upon me with ungentle looks.

3　I urg'd you further ; then you scratch'd your head,
　And too impatiently stamp'd with your foot.

4　Yet I insisted, yet you answer'd not,
　But with an angry wafter of your hand
　Gave sign for me to leave you .

5　　　　　　　　　　　　　So I did,
　Fearing to strengthen that impatience
　Which seem'd too much enkindled; and withal
　Hoping it was but an effect of humor,
　Which sometime hath his hour with every man.

6　It will not let you eat, nor talk, nor sleep;
　And could it work so much upon your shape
　As it hath much prevail'd on your {condition},
　I should not know you Brutus.

7　　　　　　　　　　　　Dear my lord,
　Make me acquainted with your cause of grief.

Portia

1   Nor for yours neither.

2   Y'have ungently Brutus
Stole from my bed : and yesternight at Supper
You sodainly arose, and walk'd about,
Musing, and sighing, with your armes a-crosse :
And when I ask'd you what the matter was,
You star'd upon me, with ungentle lookes.

3   I urg'd you further, then you scratch'd your head,
And too impatiently stampt with your foote :
Yet I insisted, yet you answer'd not,
But with an angry wafter of your hand
Gave signe for me to leave you : So I did,
Fearing to strengthen that impatience
Which seem'd too much inkindled; and withall,
Hoping it was but an effect of Humor,
Which sometime hath his houre with every man.

4   It will not let you eate, nor talke, nor sleepe;
And could it worke so much upon your shape,
As it hath much prevayl'd on your {condition},
I should not know you Brutus.

5   Deare my Lord,
Make me acquainted with your cause of greefe.

• the unembellished lines first dismiss Brutus' concerns for her health but then swiftly turn to recalling his recent disturbing and unusual actions

"Y'have ungently . . . /Stole from my bed : and yesternight . . . /You sodainly arose, and walk'd about,/Musing, and sighing, . . . /And when I ask'd you what the matter was,/You star'd upon me, ...

not only does she equally carefully describe how she pressured him for a response

"I urg'd you further, then you scratch'd your head,/And too impatiently stampt . . . /Yet I insisted, yet you answer'd not,/But with an angry wafter of your hand"

she also expresses her own responses in exactly the same way

"Fearing to strengthen that impatience/Which seem'd too much inkindled;"

as if she were still taking care not to 'strengthen that impatience' even now

• the first indication of his strange behaviour is expressed via a surround phrase

" . Y'have ungently Brutus/Stole from my bed : "

while the overall summation is via an even more impassioned monosyllabic surround phrase, formed in part by the (emotional) semicolon

" . It will not let you eate, nor talke, nor sleepe ; "

• despite Portia's unembellished care, and the speech's intellectual opening (2/0, the first two lines of the speech), after the unembellished (shock?) of his sudden walking about, she becomes emotional as she recalls asking 'what the matter was' (0/3, F #2's last three lines)

• F #3's complete catalogue of disturbing events is still emotional, but much more carefully/only occasionally released (2/4, in nine lines)

• but then her emotion gets the better of her as she sums up the effect his actions have on both of them (F #4) and in her F #5's asking to be 'acquainted with your cause of greefe' (2/7 overall in the speech's last five lines)

The Tragedie of Julius Cæsar

Portia

Brutus is wise, and were he not in health,

between 2.1.258 - 278

Background: Following on her previous speech, this is triggered by his attempt to avoid a detailed answer to her final direct request of her prior speech with a simple 'I am not well in health, and that is all'.

Style: as part of a two-handed scene

Where: in the garden of Brutus' and Portia's home

To Whom: Brutus

# of Lines: 20

Take Note: As the scene develops Portia's ability to keep herself calm begins to dissipate, as this speech clearly shows, though she does try to establish some sense of control by bringing her considerable intellect into play.

Portia

1   Brutus is wise, and were he not in health,
     He would embrace the means to come by it.

---

2   Is Brutus sick? and is it physical
     To walk unbraced and suck up the humors
     Of the dank morning?

3   What, is Brutus sick?

4   And will he steal out of his wholsome bed
     To dare the vile contagion of the night,
     And tempt the rheumy and unpurged air
     To add unto hi{s} sickness?

5   No, my Brutus,
     You have some sick offense within your mind,
     Which, by the right and virtue of my place,
     I ought to know of; and upon my knees
     I charm you, by my once commended beauty,
     By all your vows of love, and that great vow
     Which did incorporate and make us one,
     That you unfold to me, yourself, your half
     Why you are heavy ; and what men to-night
     Have had resort to you ; for here have been
     Some six or seven, who did hide their faces
     Even from darkness.

Portia

1 Brutus is wise, and were he not in health,
   He would embrace the meanes to come by it.

---

2 Is Brutus sicke?

3   And is it Physicall
   To walke unbraced, and sucke up the humours
   Of the danke Morning?

4   What, is Brutus sicke?

5 And will he steale out of his wholsome bed
   To dare the vile contagion of the Night?
   And tempt the Rhewmy, and unpurged Ayre,
   To adde unto hi{s} sicknesse?

6   No my Brutus,
   You have some sicke Offence within your minde,
   Which by the Right and Vertue of my place
   I ought to know of: And upon my knees,
   I charme you, by my once commended Beauty,
   By all your vowes of Love, and that great Vow
   Which did incorporate and make us one,
   That you unfold to me, your selfe; your halfe
   Why you are heavy : and what men to night
   Have had resort to you: for heere have beene
   Some sixe or seven, who did hide their faces
   Even from darknesse.

- as with the earlier speech that opens this scene (#20 above), in challenging Brutus yet again Portia opens very carefully (0/1, F #1), starting straightaway with the first of only two unembellished lines found
in the speech

    "Brutus is wise, and were he not in health,"

this opening care further heightened by being monosyllabic

- then, as she challenges his plea of sickness more directly than at any
earlier time in the scene, she first becomes quite emotional (3/6, F #2-
3), but finishes quite passionately (6/8, F #4-5 and the first two lines
of F #6, just five and a half lines overall) as she denies his plea, finally
accusing him of having 'some sicke Offence within your minde'

- but, as befits the daughter of a Roman Senator famous for his skills
in both debate and oratory, as she begins to demand to know 'by the
Right and Vertue of my place' (as Brutus' wife and partner) just what
is going on, her sense of control kicks in, her intellect coming to the
fore (6/2 for the next five lines)

- sadly, this does not last, for, as she baldly states her request 'That you
unfold to me, your selfe', so emotions take over fully (0/6 the remaining four and half lines of the speech) and as she defines herself
as 'your halfe' and what she wants to know, the only two surround
phrases of the speech present themselves

    " ; your halfe/Why you are heavy : and what men to night/Have
    had resort to you : "

the first underscored by being started via the emotional semicolon
(the only one in the speech), the latter further heightened by being
only the second unembellished line in the speech

The Tragedie of
Julius Cæsar

Portia

Within the Bond of Marriage, tell me Brutus,
between 2.1.280 - 302

Background: This speech is her demand for complete knowledge of what is disturbing him made full and manifest.

Style: as part of a two-handed scene

Where: in the garden of Brutus' and Portia's home

To Whom: Brutus

# of Lines: 19

Probable Timing: 1.00 minutes

Take Note: F's three separate slight onrushes (F #2, #5, and #7) show where, despite her intellect and logic, Portia's control slips, as do the three extra breath-thoughts found in the first four lines of the speech. And though F #5 is formed of five consecutive surround phrases, underscoring the strength of her determination, the fact that four of the five are in part formed by the (only) two emotional semicolons in the speech it seems that even here she has to struggle not to let her emotions get the better of her.

Portia

1   Within the bond of marriage, tell me, Brutus,
Is it excepted I should know no secrets
That appertain to you?

2   Am I your self,
But, as it were, in sort, or limitation.

3   To keep with you at meals, comfort your bed,
And talk to you sometimes?

4   Dwell I but in the suburbs
Of your good pleasure?

5   If it be no more,
Portia is Brutus' harlot, not his wife.

---

6   I grant I am a woman; but withal,
A woman that Lord Brutus took to wife.

7   I grant I am a woman; but withal,
A woman well reputed, Cato's daughter.

8   Think you I am no stronger [than] my sex,
Being so father'd and so husbanded?

9   Tell me your counsels, I will not disclose 'em.

10 I have made strong proof of my constancy,
Giving myself a voluntary wound
Here, in the thigh; can I bear that with patience,
And not my husband's secrets?

Portia

1 Within the Bond of Marriage, tell me Brutus,
Is it excepted, I should know no Secrets
That appertaine to you?

2   Am I your Selfe,
But as it were in sort, or limitation?
To keepe with you at Meales, comfort your Bed,
And talke to you sometimes?

3   Dwell I but in the Suburbs
Of your good pleasure?

4   If it be no more,
Portia is Brutus Harlot, not his Wife.

---

5 I graunt I am a Woman; but withall,
A Woman that Lord Brutus tooke to Wife:
I graunt I am a Woman; but withall,
A Woman well reputed: Cato's Daughter.

6 Thinke you, I am no stronger [then] my Sex
Being so Father'd, and so Husbanded?

7 Tell me your Counsels, I will not disclose 'em:
I have made strong proofe of my Constancie,
Giving my selfe a voluntary wound
Heere, in the Thigh: Can I beare that with patience,
And not my Husbands Secrets?

- the speech's opening argument based on the 'Bond of Marriage' is strongly intellectual (4/1, F #1), though it seems Brutus' lack of reply breaks this pattern, for the next question (whether she plays only a limited role in his life) is highly passionate (3/4, the three lines of F #2) - but this break is only momentary, for, despite the very strong imagery that follows, starting with a long (thirteen syllable line) and ending with her suggestion she is merely his 'Harlot, not his Wife', she manages to re-establish intellectual control (4/0, F #3-4)

- and it seems his lack of reply causes this pattern to break yet again, for the demanding and repetitive five consecutive surround phrase sequence forming F #5 swings back to intellectual passion yet again (9/5 in just four lines)

- though F #6's direct challenge as to her worth ('no stronger than my Sex') swings back to intellectual control (3/1), the demand seems a little difficult for her, for two extra breath-thoughts split the two line sentence into four thoughts rather than most modern texts two

- and the intellectual strength of F #7's surround phrases opening ' . Tell me your Counsels, I will not disclose 'em : ' (0/1) and the speech's final challenge " . Can I beare that with patience,/And not my Husbands Secrets ? " (3/1) only serve to illustrate how hard she is still trying to maintain self-control - even though the 'strong proofe of my Constancie' is offered passionately yet again (2/3)

The Tragedie of Julius Cæsar

Calphurnia

What mean you Cæsar?
between 2.2.8 - 54

Background: Despite the prophetic nature of both the unusually ferocious storm (see speech #1 above) and his wife's nightmares 'Thrice hath Calphurnia in her sleepe cryed out,/Helpe, ho, they murther Cæsar', Cæsar is still considering going to the Senate as planned. The following is his wife's attempt to dissuade him.

Style: as part of a two-handed scene

Where: Cæsar's home

To Whom: Cæsar

# of Lines: 23

Probable Timing: 1.10 minutes

Calpurnia

1 What mean you, Cæsar?

2   Think you to walk forth?

3 You shall not stir out of your house to-day.

---

4 {†} I never stood on ceremonies,
Yet now they fright me.

5   There is one within,
Besides the things that we have heard and seen,
Recounts most horrid sights seen by the watch.

6 A lionness hath whelped in the streets,
And graves have yawn'd and yielded up their dead;
Fierce fiery warriors fight upon the clouds
In rankes and squadrons and right form of war,
Which drizzled blood upon the Capitol;
The noise of battle hurtled in the air;
Horses [did] neigh, and dying men did groan,
And ghosts did shriek and squeal about the streets.

7 O Cæsar, these things are beyond all use,
And I do fear them.

---

8 When beggars die, there are no comets seen ;
The heavens themselves blaze forth the death of princes .

---

9 Do not go forth to day, call it my fear
That keeps you in the house, and not your own.

10 We'll send Mark Antony to the Senate-house,
And he shall say, you are not well today .

11 Let me, upon my knee, prevail in this.

Calphurnia

1　What mean you Cæsar?

2　　　　　　　　　　　　　　　Think you to walk forth?

3　You shall not stirre out of your house to day.

4　{†} I never stood on Ceremonies,
　Yet now they fright me: There is one within,
　Besides the things that we have heard and seene,
　Recounts most horrid sights seene by the Watch.

5　A Lionnesse hath whelped in the streets,
　And Graves have yawn'd, and yeelded up their dead;
　Fierce fiery Warriours fight upon the Clouds
　In Rankes and Squadrons, and right forme of Warre
　Which drizel'd blood upon the Capitoll:
　The noise of Battell hurtled in the Ayre:
　Horsses [do] neigh, and dying men did grone,
　And Ghosts did shrieke and squeale about the streets.

6　O Cæsar, these things are beyond all use,
　And I do feare them.

7　When Beggers dye, there are no Comets seen,
　The Heavens themselves blaze forth the death of Princes

　Do not go forth to day: Call it my feare,
　That keepes you in the house, and not your owne.

8　Wee'l send Mark Antony to the Senate house,
　And he shall say, you are not well to day:
　Let me upon my knee, prevaile in this.

• there are so few releases in the first three and a half lines of the speech (2/1) it seems as if Calphurnia is either so shocked by the possibility of Cæsar leaving the 'house to day' and/or is trying hard not to upset her husband that she is speaking very carefully, especially when the first three sentences are less than two lines long in total: what she has to say has to be said simply and directly without any unnecessary words or emotions

• indeed F #4's surround phrase start ' . I never stood on Ceremonies / Yet now they fright me : ' seems to suggest that she is going to be able to present her argument with a great deal of care

• but she cannot keep control, for as soon as she details all the frightening and supernatural omens that have been seen she becomes highly passionate (13/14, F #4's final two and a half lines plus the eight lines of F #5)

• two extra breath-thoughts are found in the middle of F #5, as if she needs them to continue, which in turn leads to the surround phrase marking the one item indelibly (and, as it turns out prophetically) burnt in her mind ' : The noise of Battell hurtled in the Ayre : '

• while F #6's summation of her fear maintains the passion (1/1)

• but then, a sign of her inner strength, she does regain some control, for the two line maxim opening F #7 is strongly intellectual (4/2) – but this doesn't last, for she spills without any punctuation into the monosyllabic unembellished plea 'Do not go forth to day', followed by an emotional suggestion that he blame it on her fear and 'not your owne' (1/3)

• and her final factual act seems to be a series of uncontrolled grabbing at straws, for even though F #8's first line ('Wee'l send Mark Antony to the Senate house') is intellectual, it is then followed by an unembellished one line expansion (perhaps not to anger Cæsar at the suggestion that he should send a message that he is 'not well to day'), finishing with an emotional act (kneeling) and emotional plea ('Let me . . . prevaile in this')

Ophelia

Alas my Lord, I have beene so affrighted.
between 2.1.72 - 97

Background: Despite her father's warnings, and even if she followed them to the letter, Ophelia is powerless to prevent Hamlet approaching her - which he has just done, in what seems to be a very strange manner.

Style: as part of a two-handed scene

Where: Polonius' chambers

To Whom: her father Polonius

# of Lines: 23

Probable Timing: 1.10 minutes

Take Note: While the speech is emotional overall (5/17), not surprising given the circumstances, F's orthography shows that though whatever intellectual control she may possess at the beginning of the speech quickly disappears (essentially after the first five lines), she still does not go overboard in any melodramatic way – for even when the unembellished lines evaporate after the first appearance of Hamlet has been described (F #2), the remaining twelve emotional releases are scattered throughout the last fourteen lines of the speech without any sudden unexpected outbursts.

Ophelia

1   [O] my Lord, [my lord,] I have been so affrighted !

---

2   {†} {A}s I was sewing in my [closet],
    Lord Hamlet, with his doublet all unbrac'd,
    No hat upon his head, his stockings fouled,
    Ungart'red, and down- gyved to his ankle,
    Pale as his shirt, his knees knocking each other,
    And with a look so piteous in purport
    As if he had been loosed out of hell
    To speak of horrors.   {†}

---

3   He took me by the wrist, and held me hard,
    Then goes he to the length of all his arm,
    And with his other hand thus o'er his brow,
    He falls to such perusal of my face
    As ['a] would draw it.

4   Long stay'd he so .

5   At last, a little shaking of mine arm,
    And thrice his head thus waving up and down,
    He rais'd a sigh so piteous and profound
    That it did seem to shatter all his bulk
    And end his being.

6   That done, he lets me go,
    And with his head over his [shoulder] turn'd,
    He seem'd to find his way without his eyes,
    For out [a'doors] he went without their [helps],
    And to the last bended their light on me.

Ophelia

1   [Alas] my Lord, [ ] I have beene so affrighted.

---

2   {†} {A}s I was sowing in my [Chamber],
     Lord Hamlet with his doublet all unbrac'd,
     No hat upon his head, his stockings foul'd,
     Ungartred, and downe gived to his Anckle,
     Pale as his shirt, his knees knocking each other,
     And with a looke so pitious in purport,
     As if he had been loosed out of hell,
     To speake of horrors.   {†}

---

3   He tooke me by the wrist, and held me hard;
     Then goes he to the length of all his arme;
     And with his other hand thus o're his brow,
     He fals to such perusall of my face,
     As [he] would draw it.

4   Long staid he so,
     At last, a little shaking of mine Arme:
     And thrice his head thus waving up and downe;
     He rais'd a sigh, so pittious and profound,
     That it did seeme to shatter all his bulke,
     And end his being.

5   That done, he lets me goe,
     And with his head over his [shoulders] turn'd,
     He seem'd to finde his way without his eyes,
     For out [adores] he went without their [helpe];
     And to the last, bended their light on me.

• after the first short disturbed sentence establishing her fear (F #1, 1/1) for a moment Ophelia becomes somewhat quieter (2/0 for F #2's first line and a half) in establishing Hamlet's unscheduled arrival in her 'Chamber), followed by an unembellished passage, occasionally broken by emotion (1/4), as she describes his appearance

> "with his doublet all unbrac'd,/No hat upon his head, his stockings foul'd,/ Ungartred, . . . /Pale as his shirt, his knees knocking each other,/ . . . /As if he had been loosed out of hell,"

and whether the quiet means she has managed some degree of control or that she is so frightened by what occurred that she can hardly speak about it is up to each actor to explore

• but as she describes how Hamlet held her and examined her face 'As he would draw it' her memories seem to become a little more intense, for though she continues to contain most of her emotions (0/3 in F #3's four and half lines) the effort in so doing seems to cost more, for the sentence opens with two emotional (semicoloned) surround phrases

> " . He tooke me by the wrist, and held me hard; /Then goes he to the length of all his arme; "

• the opening of F #4, how long he stayed with her and the peculiar 'waving' of his head', also seems difficult for her, for it too opens with two surround phrases

> " . Long staid he so,/At last, a little shaking of mine Arme: /And thrice his head thus waving up and downe ; "

• and as she completes the story (F #4-5) the emotions flow just a little more (1/9 in nine lines), the final moment also singled out by an emotional surround phrase

> " ; And to the last, bended their light on me . "

these last details heightened by the extra breath-thought which suggests that Ophelia is not only moved by how Hamlet behaved, but also by the fact that everything he did focused on her to the very last moment

The Tragedie of Hamlet, Prince of Denmarke

Ophelia

O what a Noble minde is heere o're-throwne?

3.1.150 - 161

Background: Not content with sending Rosincrance and Guildensterne to spy on Hamlet, to prove that spurned love for Ophelia is the cause of Hamlet's madness, Polonius and Claudius have ordered Ophelia to lay in wait for Hamlet and give him back all the gifts he sent to her, while they spy on the whole transaction. Unfortunately they have under-estimated Hamlet's current depth of psychic disturbance plus his loathing of obvious deceit, and the plan goes very awry. This speech is Ophelia's bewildered response once he has left (note how none of the descriptions in the first part of line #2 actually match sequentially the nouns in the second part of the line).

Style: solo

Where: the lobby in the castle at Elsinore

To Whom: to self and audience

# of Lines: 12

Probable Timing: 0.40 minutes

Take Note: Compared to the emotional pattern of her previous speech (5/17 in twenty-three lines), it seems that Hamlet's attack has taken her to the edge, for here she releases far more passion than ever before (20/17 in just twelve lines).

Ophelia

1   O, what a noble mind is here o'erthrown!

2   The courtier's, soldier's, scholar's, eye, tongue, sword,
     Th'[expectation] and rose of the fair state,
     The glass of fashion and the mold of form,
     Th'observ'd of all observers, quite, quite down!

3   [And] I, of ladies most deject and wretched,
     That suck'd the honey of his music vows,
     Now see that noble and most sovereign reason,
     Like sweet bells jangled out of [time], and harsh;
     That unmatch'd form and feature of blown youth
     Blasted with ecstasy.

4   O, woe is me
     T'have seen what I have seen, see what I see!

Ophelia

1   O what a Noble minde is heere o're-throwne?

2   The Courtiers, Soldiers, Schollers: Eye, tongue, sword,
Th'[expectansie] and Rose of the faire State,
The glasse of Fashion, and the mould of Forme,
Th'observ'd of all Observers, quite, quite downe.

3   [Have] I of Ladies most deject and wretched,
That suck'd the Honie of his Musicke Vowes:
Now see that Noble, and most Soveraigne Reason,
Like sweet Bels jangled out of [tune], and harsh,
That unmatch'd Forme and Feature of blowne youth,
Blasted with extasie.

4   Oh woe is me,
T'have seene what I have seene: see what I see.

- in spight of the attack, Ophelia's first (emotional, not surprisingly) thought is for Hamlet (F #1, 1/3)

- and even the intellectual start to F #2 (3/1) is still about him – though the intellect is more than somewhat disturbed since the pairings of 'Courtiers' with 'Eye', 'Soldiers' with 'tongue', and 'Schollers' with 'sword' don't match

- indeed the intellect turns to passion as she continues to bemoan what has happened to Hamlet (5/5, F #2's last three lines)

- even though describing herself as 'deject and wretched', her switch to self-focus reverts to intellect (10/5, F #3), but her intellectual stamina gives out at the last moment, for the opening of F #4's 'woe is me' is initially emotional (0/3), only to finish with an unembellished monosyllabic surround phrase ' : see what I see . ', as if all energy had finally been leached out of her

The Tragedie of Hamlet, Prince of Denmarke

Queen

One woe doth tread upon anothers heele,
between 4.7.163 - 183

Background: Laertes' anger towards Hamlet for the death of his father, and his dallying, as he sees it with Laertes sister Ophelia, (and witnessing Ophelia's last public act of madness (the herb and flower-giving) has grown exponentially. Claudius is using it to plan a second attempt on Hamlet's life when Gertrude interrupts with the following sad news.

Style: as part of a three-handed scene

Where: unspecified in the palace, perhaps Claudius' private chambers

To Whom: Laertes, in front of Claudius

# of Lines: 20

Probable Timing: 1.00 minutes

Take Note: While most modern texts present a somewhat rational Gertrude, telling Laertes the news of his sister's death in six essentially rational sentences, F shows her self-control to be much more difficult, mt. #1 and 2 originally set as the slightly onrushed F #1 (the lead-in to and the quick juxtaposition of the news of Ophelia's drowning), with the details, spread over mt. #6, jammed together in the one long seventeen and a half line F #2.

Queen

1 One woe doth tread upon another's heel,
   So fast [they] follow.

2   Your sister's drown'd, Laertes.

---

3 There is a willow grows [askant the] brook,
   That shows his [hoary] leaves in the glassy stream,
   There with fantastic garlands did she [make]
   Of crow-flowers, nettles, daisies, and long purples
   That liberal shepherds give a grosser name,
   But our cold maids do dead men's fingers call them.

4 There on the pendant boughs her coronet weeds
   Clamb'ring to hang, an envious sliver broke,
   When down the weedy Trophies and herself
   Fell in the weeping brook .

5   Her clothes spread wide,
   And mermaid-like awhile they bore her up,
   Which time she chanted snatches of old [lauds],
   As one incapable of her own distress,
   Or like a creature native and indued
   Unto that element.

6   But long it could not be
   Till that her garments, heavy with [their] drink,
   Pull'd the poor wretch from her melodious [lay]
   To muddy death.

Queen

1 One woe doth tread upon anothers heele,
   So fast [they'l] follow: your Sister's drown'd Laertes.

---

2 There is a Willow growes [aslant a] Brooke,
   That shewes his [hore] leaves in the glassie streame:
   There with fantasticke Garlands did she [come],
   Of Crow-flowers, Nettles, Daysies, and long Purples,
   That liberall Shepheards give a grosser name;
   But our cold Maids doe Dead Mens Fingers call them:
   There on the pendant boughes, her Coronet weeds
   Clambring to hang;   an envious sliver broke,
   When downe the weedy Trophies, and her selfe,
   Fell in the weeping Brooke, her cloathes spred wide,
   And Mermaid-like, a while they bore her up,
   Which time she chaunted snatches of old [tunes],
   As one incapable of her owne distresse,
   Or like a creature Native, and indued
   Unto that Element: but long it could not be,
   Till that her garments, heavy with [her] drinke,
   Pul'd the poore wretch from her melodious [buy],
   To muddy death.

- all that really need be said can be found in the two surround phrases that open the speech, F #1

> " . One woe doth tread upon anothers heele,/So fast [they'l] follow: your Sister's drown'd Laertes ."

the first emotional (0/1), the information of the second strictly factual (2/0)

- at first the only two other surround phrases seem unnecessary

> " ; But our cold Maids doe Dead Mens Fingers call them : /There on the pendant boughes, her Coronet weeds/Clambring to hang ; "

yet the semicolons (suggesting great emotion) and the second phrase, beginning to explain how Ophelia came to fall in the water, point to the extreme strain Gertrude is under, with the first phrase perhaps an attempt to put off (or ready herself) having to speak about the actual drowning

- in establishing the what and where of the new 'woe' the speech starts passionately (4/4 the first four lines), while the details of the 'Garlands' of flowers Ophelia was weaving are handled much more factually (10/5, F #2's lines three to six, to the second colon)

- in describing Ophelia's 'Clambring' on to the 'pendant boughes' and falling into the 'weeping Brooke', Gertrude becomes passionate once more (3/4, F #2's lines seven to ten) while the remainder of the speech, right up to the point of 'muddy death', is gently emotional (2/5, the last seven lines), the only intellectual digression being when Gertrude elaborates the earlier 'Mermaid-like' image of Ophelia as seeming to belong to the water 'like a creature Native, and indued/ Unto that Element'

The Tragedie of Troylus and Cressida

Cressida

Words, vowes, gifts, teares, & loves full sacrifice,
1.2.282 - 295

Background: though young, Cressida shows her understanding of the world in general, and especially its sexual machinations – indeed just before this speech she has had a wit-duel with her uncle: now he's gone she reveals her innermost thoughts to the audience

Style: initially with possibly one other present, and then solo

Where: outdoors, somewhere near the gates of Troy

To Whom: perhaps her man Alexander is still present at the top of the speech, and then to audience and self

# of Lines: 14

Probable Timing: 0.45 minutes

Take Note: In what is a very adult assessment and some would argue cynical view of love it is not surprising that Cressida is essentially emotional (4/14 overall), the calm of the unembellished lines and the determined assessments of the surround phrases pointing to the depth of her understanding. Yet the onrush of F #1-2, and the reworking of F #3 (longer than the mt. equivalent) and F #4 (shorter) suggest she is not quite as calm as the words and orthography alone would indicate.

Cressida

1   Words, vows, gifts, tears, [and] love's full sacrifice,
     He offers in another's enterprise.

2   But more in Troilus thousand fold I see
     [Than] in the glass of Pandar's praise may be;
     Yet hold I off.

3   Women are angels, wooing:
     Things won are done, joy's soul lies in the doing.

4   That she belov'd, knows nought that knows not this:
     Men prize the thing ungain'd more [than] it is.

5   That she was never yet that ever knew
     Love got so sweet, as when desire did sue.

6   Therefore this maxim out of love I teach:
     "Achievement, is command; ungain'd, beseech";
     [Then] though my heart's [content] firm love doth bear,
     Nothing of that shall from mine eyes appear

Cressida

1　Words, vowes, gifts, teares, & loves full sacrifice,
He offers in anothers enterprise :
But more in Troylus thousand fold I see,
[Then] in the glasse of Pandar's praise may be ;
Yet hold I off.

2　　　Women are Angels wooing,
Things won are done, joyes soule lyes in the dooing :
That she belov'd, knowes nought, that knowes not this ;
Men prize the thing ungain'd, more [then] it is.

3　That she was never yet, that ever knew
Love got so sweet, as when desire did sue :
Therefore this maxime out of love I teach ;
"Atchievement, is command; ungain'd, beseech.

4　[That] though my hearts [Contents] firme love doth beare,
Nothing of that shall from mine eyes appeare.

• thus it's fascinating that the only intellectual moment concerns her obvious admiration of Troylus (F #1's last two and a half lines), and that the most released emotional moment is in her expression of the dilemma of 'joyes soule lyes in the dooing' versus what every woman 'knowes', that men do not prize what is easily won (0/6 in the second and third lines of F #2)

• the surround phrases underscore the very clear thoughts that currently drive Cressida not to accept Pandarus' surface blandishments, and why

> " ; Yet hold I off."

> " . Women are Angels wooing, /Things won are done, joyes soule lyes in the dooing : /That she belov'd, knowes nought, that knowes not this ; /Men prize the thing ungain'd, more then it is ."

> " . Therefore this maxime out of love I teach ; /Atchievement, is command ; ungain'd, beseech . "

• while the calm of the unembellished lines demonstrates a surprisingly clear understanding for one so young of manipulations in the name of love, first dismissing Pandarus because

> "He offers in anothers enterprise:"

then neatly and effortlessly skewering the superficiality of men's desires

> "Men prize the thing ungain'd, more then it is./That she was never yet, that ever knew/Love got so sweet, as when desire did sue:"

The Tragedie of
Troylus and Cressida

Cressida

Boldnesse comes to mee now, and brings mee
between 3.2.113 - 133

Background: Cressida finally confesses to Troylus how she has felt about him - though whether she is behaving genuinely or behaving archly is up to each actress and production to decide

Style: as part of a three-handed scene

Where: just outside where Cressida lives

To Whom: to Troylus in front of her uncle Pandarus

# of Lines: 20

Probable Timing: 1.00 minutes

Take Note: Cressida's emotionality (4/17 overall) and the fact that the first twelve lines of the speech are all made up of surround phrases, together with F/Q's transition from #1's prose to #2's verse (see below) reinforces the idea of a lady not at all sure of herself, and working very hard to get her thoughts across, at least at the beginning of the speech. However, the large number of unembellished lines among the surround phrases, and continuing thereafter , suggests that what she does have to say she often says with quiet dignity (whether out of embarrassment or quiet conviction is for each actor to explore).

Cressida

1　Boldness comes to me now, and brings me heart .

2　Prince Troilus , I have lov'd you night and day
　For many weary months.

3　Hard to seem won ;　but I was won, my lord,
　With the first glance that ever - pardon me,
　If I confess much, you will play the tyrant .

4　I love you now, but [till not now] so much
　But I might master it .

5　　　　　　　　　　　　　In faith I lie ,
　My thoughts were like unbridled children [grown]
　Too head-strong for their mother .

6　　　　　　　　　　　　　　See, we fools!
　Why have I blabb'd ?

7　　　　　　　　　　　Who shall be true to us,
　When we are so unsecret to ourselves ?

8　But though I lov'd you well, I wooed you not,
　And yet, good faith, I wish'd myself a man,
　Or that we women had men's privilege
　Of speaking first.

9　　　　　　　　　Sweet, bid me hold my tongue,
　For in this rapture I shall surely speak
　The thing I shall repent .

10　　　　　　　　　　See, see, your silence,
　[Cunning] in dumbness, from my weakness draws
　My soul of counsel [ ] !

　　11　　　　　　　　　Stop my mouth .

Cressida

1   Boldnesse comes to mee now, and brings mee
    heart : Prince Troylus, I have lov'd you night and day, for
    many weary moneths.

---

2   Hard to seeme won :   but I was won my Lord
    With the first glance ;   that ever pardon me,
    If I confesse much you will play the tyrant :
    I love you now, but [not till now] so much
    But I might maister it ;   infaith I lye :
    My thoughts were like unbrideled children [grow]
    Too head-strong for their mother :   see we fooles,
    Why have I blab'd :   who shall be true to us
    When we are so unsecret to our selves?

3   But though I lov'd you well, I woed you not,
    And yet good faith I wisht my selfe a man ;
    Or that we women had mens priviledge
    Of speaking first.

4   Sweet, bid me hold my tongue,
    For in this rapture I shall surely speake
    The thing I shall repent :   see, see, your silence
    [Comming] in dumbnesse, from my weakenesse drawes
    My soule of counsell [from me].

5   Stop my mouth

- the opening line is highly emotional (0/3) and though Q/F set the slightly onrushed F #1 as prose, thus adding to the idea of it being an awkward start for Cressida, most modern texts set their more rational equivalent mt. #1-2 as verse as shown, thus removing the transition when she finally summons up enough strength to move into the heightened awareness that verse usually suggests

- then in the second line of F #2/mt. #3 most modern texts create an awkwardness not shown in F: F allows Cressida a certain dignity in setting an emotional, (via the semicolon) but clear, quiet, unembellished explanation acknowledging her forwardness at falling in love 'With the first glance ; that ever pardon me,': most modern texts repunctuate this to 'With the first glance that ever - pardon me,' setting up a much more fumbling apology, undermining the independent young woman that was seen in speech #3 above

- other unembellished lines offer further examples of her dignity under pressure, 'I love you now, but not till now so much . . .'; and the three consecutive lines

    "Why have I blab'd : who shall be true to us/When we are so unsecret to our selves?/But though I lov'd you well, I woed you not,"

together with the monosyllabic opening to F #4 'Sweet, bid me hold my tongue,' and her final request, 'Stop my mouth.'

- the most emotional moment in an already emotional speech comes in F #4's last two lines when she chides both him for his silence and herself for giving too much away 'see, see, your silence/[Cunning] in dumbnesse, from my weaknesse drawes/My soule of counsell from me.' (0/6), while the only time capitals are seen is in her early formal address to him as 'Prince Troylus' (the second line of F #10)

The Tragedie of
Troylus and Cressida

Cressida

O you immortall gods! I will not goe.
between 4.4.85 -108

Background: the exchange of Cressida (to go to join her father in the
Greek camp) in return for the captured Trojan Antenor has been
arranged, and is to take place immediately, the very night she and
Troylus have just become lovers: the task of collecting her has been
delegated to a Trojan commander, Æneas, who in turn has left it to
Pandarus to tell her she must go: the following is her immediate reply

Style: perhaps part of a four-handed scene, with (perhaps) Troylus and
Æneas in nearby attendance, though a two-handed scene is more likely

Where: just outside where Cressida lives

To Whom: to her uncle Pandarus

# of Lines: 14

Probable Timing: 0.45 minutes

Take Note: Not surprisingly given the news that she must leave Troylus
immediately, overall the speech seems highly emotional (8/17 in just
fourteen lines) yet apart from the first two incredibly short sentences of protest (0/2) and the protest she knows 'no bloud, no soule, so
neere me,' (0/3) Cressida manages to contain her emotions and maintain a great deal of self control in the first half of the speech (7/2, the
other eight and a half lines, including the incredibly quiet denial of
her father 'I know no touch of consanguinitie').

Cressida

1   O you immortal gods!

2   I will not go.

---

3   I will not, uncle.

4   I have forgot my father,
    I know no touch of consanguinity;
    No kin, no love, no blood, no soul, so near me
    As the sweet Troilus :   O you gods divine!

5   Make Cressid's name the very crown of falsehood,
    If ever she leave Troilus !

6   Time, force and death,
    Do to this body what [extremes] you can ;
    But the strong base and building of my love
    Is as the very center of the earth,
    Drawing all things to it.

7   [I'll] go in and weep{,}

Tear my bright [hair], and scratch my praised cheeks,
Crack my clear voice with sobs, and break my heart,
With sounding Troilus .

8   I will not go from Troy.

Cressida

1   O you immortall gods!

2   I will not goe.

---

3   I will not Unckle: I have forgot my Father:
I know no touch of consanguinitie:
No kin, no love, no bloud, no soule, so neere me,
As the sweet Troylus: O you gods divine!
Make Cressids name the very crowne of falshood!
If ever she leave Troylus: time, {f}orce and death,
Do to this body what extremitie you can;
But the strong base and building of my love,
Is as the very Center of the earth,
Drawing all things to it.

4   I will goe in and weepe{,}

Teare my bright heire, and scratch my praised cheekes,
Cracke my cleere voyce with sobs, and breake my heart
With sounding Troylus.

5   I will not goe from Troy.

- the already passionate opening is enhanced by the rare (for an original Shakespeare printing) exclamation mark (F #1)

- her determination not leave Troy and Troylus is enhanced by the three surround phrases that open F #3

> " . I will not Unckle : I have forgot my Father : /I know no touch of consanguinitie : "

while the pain of having to break her promise not to leave Troylus

> " : O you gods divine! /Make Cressids name the very crowne of falshood! /If ever she leave Troylus : time, force and death,/ Do to this body what extremitie you can ; "

is similarly intensified, and highlighted even more by the surround phrases, two more exclamation marks, and an emotional semicolon, with last two heightened even further by being unembellished (save for the name of Troylus)

- and then, save for the all-important 'Center' come three more unembellished lines proclaiming the strength of her love (it seems she is determined all who hear her should be impressed by her intense calmness) to end F #3

- but then with the dreadful tug of 'I will . . weepe' versus 'I will teare my bright [heire] and scratch my praised cheekes' versus 'I will not goe from Troy.', her emotions finally get the better of her, (2/10 the speech's last three and a half lines, F #4-5)

The Tragedie of Troylus and Cressida

Cassandra

Cry Troyans cry;   lend me ten thousand eyes,
between 2.2.101 - 112

Background: known as a prophetess, Cassandra the only one of Priam's daughters shown in the play, bursts in on the family with her very dark visions

Style: group address

Where: unspecified, but probably in the family private chambers

To Whom: her father Priam, and brothers Hector, Troylus, Paris and Helenus

# of Lines: 11

Probable Timing: 0.40 minutes

Take Note: The rational nine sentence structure offered by most modern texts in no way reflects the onrush of F's four sentences or the fact that both F's opening and closing sentences, and the opening of F #2 are all incredibly heightened by being formed by emotional (semicoloned) surround phrases (five in all).

Cassandra

1 Cry, Troyans, cry ! lend me ten thousand eyes,
   And I will fill them with prophetic tears.

2 Virgins, and boys, mid-age & wrinkled [eld],
   Soft infancy, that nothing [canst] but cry,
   Add to my [clamors] !

3   Let us pay betimes
   A moi'ty of that mass of moan to come.

4 Cry, Troyans, cry !, practice your eyes with tears!

5 Troy must not be, nor goodly Ilion stand.

6 Our fire-brand brother Paris burns us all.

7 Cry, Troyans, cry !, a Helen and a woe !

8 Cry, cry !

9   Troy burns, or else let Helen go.

Cassandra

1   Cry Troyans cry;   lend me ten thousand eyes,
And I will fill them with Propheticke teares.

---

2   Virgins, and Boyes;   mid-age & wrinkled old,
Soft infancie, that nothing [can] but cry,
Adde to my [clamour]:   let us pay betimes
A moity of that masse of moane to come.

3   Cry Troyans cry, practise your eyes with teares,
Troy must not be, nor goodly Illion stand,
Our fire-brand Brother Paris burnes us all.

4   Cry Troyans cry, a Helen and a woe;
Cry, cry, Troy burnes, or else let Helen goe.

- F #1's emotional surround phrase opening invocation ' . Cry Troyans cry ; ' eventually becomes passionate (2/2), though interestingly the bulk of the release doesn't occur until the sentence end - 'Propheticke teares', as if, at the very last, she cannot contain herself, and the release now turns to emotion, the surround phrases of the ensuing F #2 (1/3) spelling out who should mourn and how, ' . Virgins and Boyes ; . . . : let us pay betimes/A moity of that masse of moane to come . '

- but then very surprisingly Cassandra seems to take hold of herself, for despite the unrelenting appalling clarity of her images, the warning/ prophecy of her next five lines (F #3 and the first of F #4) are strongly factual (6/2)

- placing Helen as the cause of Troy's forthcoming losses releases her emotions once more, for the two surround phrases forming this last sentence (F #4) are linked by an emotional semicolon

- which in turn leads to a final passionate plea/warning of the last line 'Troy burnes, or else let Helen goe.' (2/2 in just seven words)

The Tragedie of Othello, the Moore ov Venice

Desdemona

{Nor would I at home} recide,
between 1.3.241 - 259

Background: Othello has taken the unusual step of asking that Desdemona, his new wife and Brabantio's daughter, be allowed to give witness in and to the Senate on the charges of witchcraft brought by Brabantio against Othello: in this speech Desdemona makes a plea to the Duke to be allowed to accompany Othello to the war in Cyprus, triggered by the initial suggestion from the Duke that while Othello is away she reside 'at her Fathers', a suggestion immediately rejected by both Brabantio and Othello

Style: one on one address in front of a larger group

Where: the Senate chamber

To Whom: the Duke, in front of Othello, Brabantio, and the Senators at large

# of Lines: 18

Probable Timing: 0.55 minutes

Desdemona

1   Nor [I, I would not] {at home} reside,
     To put my father in impatient thoughts
     By being in his eye.

2   Most gracious Duke,
     To my unfolding, lend [a gracious] ear,
     And let me find a charter in your voice
     T'assist my simpleness.

---

3   That I [did] love the Moor to live with him,
     My downright violence, and storm of fortunes,
     May trumpet to the world.

4   My heart's subdu'd
     Even to the very quality of my Lord.

5   I saw Othello's visage in his mind,
     And to his honors and his valiant parts
     Did I my soul and fortunes consecrate.

6   So that, dear lords, if I be left behind,
     A moth of peace, and he go to the war,
     The rites for [which] I love him are bereft me,
     And I a heavy interim shall support
     By his dear absence.

7   Let me go with him.

Desdemona

1   Nor [ ] [would I] {at home} recide,
    To put my Father in impatient thoughts
    By being in his eye.

2   Most Gracious Duke,
    To my unfolding, lend [your prosperous] eare,
    And let me finde a Charter in your voice
    T'assist my simplenesse.

---

3   That I [ ] love the Moore, to live with him,
    My downe-right violence, and storme of Fortunes
    May trumpet to the world.

4   My heart's subdu'd
    Even to the very quality of my Lord;
    I saw Othello's visage in his mind,
    And to his Honours and his valiant parts,
    Did I my soule and Fortunes consecrate.

5   So that (deere Lords) if I be left behind
    A Moth of Peace and he go to the Warre,
    The Rites for [why] I love him, are bereft me:
    And I a heavie interim shall support
    By his deere absence.

6   Let me go with him.

- the foundation for Desdemona's love is shown by the only emotional semicolon in the speech which connects the surround phrase ' . My heart's subdu'd/Even to the very quality of my Lord ; ' to the key statement that follows, 'I saw Othello's visage in his mind,'

- F #1's denial of the Duke's suggestion (that she stay at her father's while Othello takes up duty in Cyprus) is carefully expressed (1/0)

- yet she becomes very passionate (for the first time since she came on-stage) in her plea to be heard (in what is going to be a virtually unprecedented request) – to be allowed to go to war with Othello (F #2, 3/3)

- and this passion continues as she begins to explain why, starting with an unequivocal statement of her love for Othello (F #3, 3/2)

- starting with the surround phrase discussed above, her explanation of why she loves him and the statement she has consecrated her 'soule and Fortunes' to him while still passionate become slightly more intellectual (4/2, F #4), and her statement that she doesn't want to be left behind as a 'Moth of Peace' is even more so (5/2, F #5), the final explanation

    " : And I a heavie interim shall support/By his deere absence. "

heightened by being set as the only logical surround phrase in the speech

- finally, Desdemona's self-controlled dignity (remarkable for one so young, and important for the rest of the play) is clearly seen in F #6's extraordinarily simple and unequivocal summation/request, ' . Let me go with him.' – a dignity triply enhanced by being set as a short sentence which is monosyllabic and unembellished

The Tragedie of Othello, the Moore of Venice

Æmilia

Goodmorrow (good Lieutenant) I am sorrie
between 3.1.41 - 55

Background: following Iago's advice (speech #12 immediately above), Cassio has gone to Desdemona's companion Æmilia (Iago's wife) to ask for her help in getting him access to Desdemona: the following is her reply, her first major speech in the play

Style: as part of a two-handed scene

Where: somewhere in the garrison

To Whom: Cassio

# of Lines: 12

Probable Timing: 0.40 minutes

Take note: In a speech where the metrical irregularity suggests concern the orthographic inconsistency Æmilia shows after F #1 suggests a woman who is finding it difficult, for whatever reason, to maintain self-control.

Æmilia

1   Good morrow, good lieutenant .

2   I am sorry
    For your displeasure; but all will [soon] be well.

3   The general and his wife are talking of it,
    And she speaks for you stoutly.

4   The Moor replies,
    That he you hurt is of great fame in Cyprus,
    And great affinity; and that in wholesome wisdom
    He might not but refuse you.

5   But he protests he loves you,
    And needs no other suitor but his likings
    [To take the safest occasion by the front]
    To bring you in again.

---

6   Pray you come in.

7   I will bestow you where you shall have time
    To speak your bosom freely.

Æmilia

1 Goodmorrow (good Lieutenant) I am sorrie
  For your displeasure: but all will [sure] be well.

2 The Generall and his wife are talking of it,
  And she speakes for you stoutly.

3   The Moore replies,
  That he you hurt is of great Fame in Cyprus,
  And great Affinitie: and that in wholsome Wisedome
  He might not but refuse you.

4   But he protests he loves you
  And needs no other Suitor, but his likings
  [ ]
  To bring you in againe.

---

5   Pray you come in:
  I will bestow you where you shall have time
  To speake your bosome freely.

• F #1's opening intellectual surround phrases (1/0), including the unembellished

> " . . . I am sorrie/For your displeasure : but all will sure be well . "

point to a very careful opening (considering Iago's suspicions about Æmilia and Cassio, even if they are not lovers it could well be that she is carrying a torch for him and doesn't want to give herself away) - but then come the inconsistencies

• the fact that Cassio is being talked about is emotional (1/2, F #2); the fact that the man he has hurt is of 'great Fame . . ./And great Affinitie' is intellectual (4/1, the first two lines of F #3), while the end to F #3, explaining Othello

> " : and that in wholsome Wisedome/He might not but refuse you . "

is heightened by being set as an emotional surround phrase (1/2)

• then comes another unembellished phrase, F #4's opening 'But he protests he loves you', the quietness seeming to suggest a very care-ful (delicate) reassurance – whether because of Cassio's distress or a genuine belief is up to each actor to decide – yet the explanation is passionate once more(1/1)

• and so comes an extended unembellished passage to open F #5, 'Pray you come in : /I will bestow you where you shall have time . . . ", (and whether the quiet and the surround phrase start are a further reminder of Æmilia's fondness, or simply genuine empathy is again up to each actor to decide)

• the speech's last line finishes emotionally (0/2)

The Tragedie of Othello, the Moore of Venice

Desdemona

Do not doubt Cassio/But I will have my Lord, and you againe
between 3.3.5 - 28

Background: as Cassio (and Iago) hoped once Desdemona is asked to intercede with to get Cassio reinstated as Othello's lieutenant, she goes at it whole-heartedly: this speech is her promise to Cassio

Style: part of a three-handed scene

Where: unspecified, but somewhere in the garrison or its gardens at Cyprus

To Whom: Cassio, in front of Æmilia

# of Lines: 15

Probable Timing: 0.50 minutes

Take Note: F's orthography beautifully reveals the two sides of Desdemona, her controlled dignity, and her delightful exuberance, and how quickly she can move from one mood to another.

Desdemona

1   Do not doubt, Cassio,
    But I will have my lord, and you again
    As friendly as you were.

---

2   You do love my lord;
    You have known him long, and be you well assur'd
    He shall in strangeness stand no farther off
    [Than] in a politic distance.

---

3   Do not doubt {†}; before Emilia here,
    I give thee warrant of thy place.

4   Assure thee,
    If I do vow a friendship, I'll perform it
    To the last article.

5   My lord shall never rest,
    I'll watch him tame, and talk him out of patience;
    His bed shall seem a school, his board a shrift,
    I'll intermingle every thing he does
    With Cassio's suit.

6   Therefore be merry, Cassio,
    For thy solicitor shall rather die
    [Than] give thy cause away.

Desdemona

1　　　Do not doubt Cassio
　　But I will have my Lord, and you againe
　　As friendly as you were.

2　　　　　　　　　　You do love my Lord:
　　You have knowne him long, and be you well assur'd
　　He shall in strangenesse stand no farther off,
　　[Then] in a politique distance.

3　Do not doubt {†}:　before Æmilia here,
　I give thee warrant of thy place.

4　　　　　　　　　　　Assure thee,
　　If I do vow a friendship, Ile performe it
　　To the last Article.

5　　　　　My Lord shall never rest,
　　Ile watch him tame, and talke him out of patience;
　　His Bed shall seeme a Schoole, his Boord a Shrift,
　　Ile intermingle every thing he do's
　　With Cassio's suite:　Therefore be merry Cassio,
　　For thy Solicitor shall rather dye,
　　[Then] give thy cause away.

• the surround phrases highlight the very clear logic of what she is prepared to do for Cassio, and her rationale, from F #2's opening monosyllabic

> ' . You do love my Lord : "

through to F #3's

> " . Do not doubt : before Æmilia here, / I give thee warrant of thy place . "

to F #5's opening

> " . My Lord shall never rest, / Ile watch him tame, and talke him out of patience ; "

the emotional semicolon of the latter perhaps suggesting a youthful anticipation (joy? fun? mischief? delight?) of what may come

• F #1's opening reassurance to Cassio that he and Othello will soon be friends again is slightly passionate (2/1), which then turns to emotion in the F #2 promise that Othello shall only stand off from Cassio 'a politique distance' (1/3)

• in its virtually unembellished calm, F #3 shows great dignity, her determination enhanced by two surround phrases as she gives Cassio 'warrant of thy place' (0/1),

• and the calm determination is continued into F #4, her unembellished statement ' Assure thee, / If I do vow a friendship,' with what she promises ('My Lord shall never rest,') becoming passionate (2/2 the last line of F #4 and the first line and a half of F #5)

• the promises having been made, the emotional semicolon releases a sudden onrushed flurry of intellectual and emotional verbiage (8/5 the speech's last four and a half lines) as she pictures just where (mainly it seems Othello's 'Bed') she shall plead for Cassio and the, to her, inevitable happy outcome

The Tragedie of Othello,
the Moore of Venice

Bianca

'**Save you (Friend Cassio.)**
between 3.4.169 – 187

Background: arriving in Cyprus, Cassio took up with the courtesan, Bianca, though since his firing and reinstatement he has taken care to see much less of her than before, hence this speech: Iago can use this relationship to poison Othello's mind even further, especially since later on Bianca produces the missing magical handkerchiefe in front of the hidden Othello, thus confirming Cassio's possession of it

Style: part of a two-handed scene

Where: in a Cyprus street

To Whom: Cassio

20/ # of Lines: 12

Probable Timing: 0.40 minutes

Bianca

1 'Save you , friend Cassio !

---

2 {†} I was {coming} to your lodging,{†}.

3 What? keep a week away? seven days and nights?

4 Eightscore eight hours? and lovers' absent hours,
More tedious [than] the dial, eightscore times?

5 O weary reck'ning !

---

6 {W}hence came this{handkerchief}?

7 {You} found it in {your} chamber .

8 {You} like the work well; ere it be demanded
(As like enough it will) {you} would have it copied .

9 Take it, and do't, and leave {you} for this time {?}

---

10 This is some token from a newer friend ;
To the felt-absence now I feel a cause.

11 Is't come to this?

12 [ ]

---

13 {W}ho's is it?

Bianca

1　'Save you (Friend Cassio.)

2　{†} I was {coming} to your Lodging,{†}.

3　What? keepe a weeke away?

4　　　　　　　　　　　　　　　Seven dayes, and Nights?

5　Eight score eight houres?

6　　　　　　　　　　　　And Lovers absent howres
　　More tedious [then] the Diall, eight score times?

7　Oh weary reck'ning.

8　　　　　　　　　　　{W}hence came this {handkerchiefe}?

9　{You} found it in {your} Chamber,
　{You} like the worke well; Ere it be demanded
　(As like enough it will) {you} would have it coppied:
　Take it, and doo't, and leave {you} for this time{?}

10　This is some Token from a newer Friend,
　　To the felt-Absence: now I feele a Cause:
　　Is't come to this?

11　　　　　　　　　　　[Well, well.]

12　　　　　　　　　　　　{W}ho's is it?

• the speech opens quite factually (F #1-2, 3/0) perhaps suggesting a moment of care from a kept woman meeting her soldier/lover in a public space

• but then comes Bianca's emotional (seductive perhaps) reprimand for his staying away from her for a week (1/4, F #3-5), the approach heightened in being set as three short sentences – as if each were sufficient in and of itself to get some form of response, verbal or otherwise

• and as the implied sexual heat turns up a notch ('Lovers absent howres') so Bianca becomes passionate (3/4, F #6-7)

• however, once the 'handkerchiefe' is produced for her to copy her manner changes – first becoming emotional both in release (2/4, F #8-9), and with the appearance of surround phrases, the first two linked by the only emotional semicolon in the speech

" {You} found it in {your} Chamber,/{You} like the worke well ; Ere it be

demanded/(As like enough it will) {you} would have it coppied :

/Take it, and doo't, and leave {you} for this time {?} "

the firm challenging logic of the latter heightened by being monosyllabic

• then as she challenges Cassio to tell her where it came from (suspecting 'a newer Friend') so her intellect sweeps in (4/1, F #10's first two lines), the demand of the sentence intensified by being set as thee more logical surround phrases

• and after all the releases Bianca ends very (quietly dangerously so?)

" ; Is't come to this ? Well, well. {Who's} is it?"

the unembellished calm doubly heightened by being monosyllabic and set either via a surround phrase (F #10) or two very short sentences (F #11-12)

The Tragedie of Othello,
the Moore of Venice

Desdemona

I prythee do {go meet him} . Something sure of State,
3.4.140 - 154

Background: finally Desdemona asks Iago to go to intercede with him on her behalf

Style: as part of a three-handed scene

Where: close to Othello's private chambers within the garrison

To Whom: Iago, in front of Æmilia

# of Lines: 14

Probable Timing: 0.45 minutes

Take Note: That the situation may be slowly becoming too much for Desdemona to maintain her previously displayed self-control at times of stress can be seen in that while her intellect predominates in searching for a political/military/matters of state reason for Othello's sudden change of behaviour (5/2, F #1-3), so emotion (2/6, F #4-5) and passion (4/4, F #6) swamp her, once she believes she has found one.

Desdemona

1   I prithee do {go meet him}.

2   Something sure of state,
     Either from Venice, or some unhatch'd practice
     Made demonstrable here in Cyprus to him,
     Hath puddled his clear spirit; and in such cases
     Men's natures wrangle with inferior things,
     Though great ones are [the] object.

3   'Tis even so;
     For let our finger ache, and it endues
     Our other healthful members, even to [that] sense
     Of pain.

4   Nay, we must think men are not gods,
     Nor of them look for such [observances]
     As fits the bridal.

5   Beshrew me much, Emilia,
     I was (unhandsome warrior as I am)
     Arraigning his unkindness with my soul;
     But now I find I had subborn'd the witness,
     And he's indicted falsely.

Desdemona

1   I prythee do {go meet him}.

2   Something sure of State,
     Either from Venice, or some unhatch'd practise
     Made demonstrable heere in Cyprus, to him,
     Hath pudled his cleare Spirit: and in such cases,
     Mens Natures wrangle with inferiour things,
     Though great ones are [their] object.

3   'Tis even so.

4   For let our finger ake, and it endues
     Our other healthfull members, even to [a] sense
     Of paine.

5   Nay, we must thinke men are not Gods,
     Nor of them looke for such [observancie]
     As fits the Bridall.

6   Beshrew me much, Æmilia,
     I was (unhandsome Warrior, as I am)
     Arraigning his unkindnesse with my soule:
     But now I finde, I had suborn'd the Witnesse,
     And he's Indited falsely.

• her determined attempt to maintain self-control might well be seen in the opening unembellished short sentence request for Iago to go to Othello (F #1)

• and the immediate sense of relief when she believes she has found an answer might be seen in the quiet of the even shorter unembellished F #3, ' 'Tis even so.'

• while the passionate blaming of her self for, as she now thinks, her faulty understanding not worthy of her own view of herself as a 'Warrior', (4/4, F #6) is heightened by the only surround phrase in the speech

> " : But now I finde, I had suborn'd the Witnesse,/And he's Indited falsely . "

her self-denigration made even stronger by being the last words of the speech

• what might be somewhat unexpected is the F #4 emotion (0/3) with which she tries to justify Othello's taking out on her what she believes is a problem either from Venice or from his presence in Cyprus, and also F #5's passion (2/3) with which she suggests it might be better if women realised first that men are not Gods (and therefore should not expect them to withstand serious distractions), and that they cannot always behave (with as much courtesy?) as they do when they are making love

The Tragedie of Macbeth

Lady Macbeth/Lady

They met me in the day of successe : and I have

1.5.1 - 14

Background: These are Lady Macbeth's (referred to in the first folio simply as 'Lady') first series of speeches in the play, all triggered by a letter from her husband telling her of the strange greetings and prophecies, including that of becoming King. This speech deals with the letter itself (the italics being a conventional First Folio method of setting written documents.

Style: solo

Where: somewhere in the castle at Inverness, possibly her private chambers

To Whom: self

# of Lines: 12

Probable Timing: 0.40 minutes

Take Note: Her immediate response to the various stages of information the letter presents her suggests that she is reading it for the first time or is at last alone where she can read it aloud and react to it for the first time - and though the overall speech seems passionate (10/10 overall), each piece of news seems to bring a different stylistic response.

Lady Macbeth

1   "They met me in the day of success; and I have
learn'd by the perfect'st report, they have more in them, [than]
mortal˙ knowledge .

2   When I burnt in desire to question them further,
they made themselves air, into which they vanish'd .

3   Whiles I stood rapt in the wonder of it, came missives from
the King, who all-hail'd me 'Thane of Cawdor,' by which
title, before, these [weird˙] sisters saluted me, and referr'd
me to the coming˙ on of time, with 'Hail˙, King that shalt be!'

4   This
have I thought good to deliver thee, my dearest partner of
greatness, that thou mightst not lose the dues of
rejoicing by being ignorant of what greatness is promis'd
thee .

5   Lay it to thy heart, and farewell ."

Lady

*1   They met me in the day of successe: and I have
learn'd by the perfect'st report, they have more in them, [then]
mortall knowledge.*

*2   When I burnt in desire to question them
further, they made themselves Ayre, into which they vanish'd.*

*3   Whiles I stood rapt in the wonder of it, came Missives from
the King, who all hail'd me Thane of Cawdor, by which Title
before, these [weyward] Sisters saluted me, and referr'd me to
the comming on of time, with haile King that shalt be .*

*4   This
have I thought good to deliver thee (my dearest Partner of
Greatnesse) that thou might'st not loose the dues of rejoycing
by being ignorant of what Greatnesse is promis'd thee .*

*5   Lay
it to thy heart, and farewell.*

- given the circumstances, it's hardly surprising that she starts emotionally (F #1, 0/2), yet - a wonderful sign of her strength of mind throughout - she opens carefully, with two of the first four phrases being unembellished

  > "and I have learn'd by the perfect'st report, they have more in them,"

and the surround phrase that opens the reading of the letter

  > ' . They met me in the day of successe ; '

suggesting great concentration

- and she remains calm with the information that the Weyward Sisters just disappeared, for with the exception of the 'Ayre' they vanished into, this is also unembellished (F #2, 1/1)

- then her mind becomes very active as she processes how 'Missives from the King' confirmed the 'Thane of Cawdor' (6/0, F #3's first three lines) – at least until she reads the prophecy that Macbeth will be 'King', at which point the first emotion kicks in (1/2, F #3's last line)

- and so comes passion (3/4, F #4) as she reads Macbeth's confirmation that she is now and will in the future be 'my dearest Partner of Greatnesse'

- that the last sentence is unembellished is surprising, perhaps suggesting that the news and/or her immediate reaction to it has almost taken her breath away

The Tragedie of Macbeth

Lady Macbeth/Lady

Glamys thou art, and Cawdor, and shalt be
1.5.15 - 30

Background: In this speech Lady Macbeth unflinchingly faces what weaknesses must be overcome if Macbeth is to become king.

Style: all solo

Where: somewhere in the castle at Inverness, possibly her private chambers

To Whom: self

Take Note: It is only after much husband-character-analysis and having found the approach 'To have thee crown'd withall', that her passions finally flow.

# of Lines: 17

Probable Timing: 0.55 minutes

Lady Macbeth

1   [Glamis] thou art, and Cawdor, and shalt be
    What thou art promis'd.

2   Yet do I fear thy nature,
    It is too full o'th'milk of [human] kindness
    To catch the nearest way.

3   Thou wouldst be great,
    Art not without ambition, but without
    The illness should attend it.

4   What thou wouldst highly,
    That wouldst thou holily; wouldst not play false,
    And yet wouldst wrongly win.

5   Thou'ldst have, great[Glamis],
    That which cries, "*Thus thou must do, if thou have it*;"
    And that which rather thou dost fear to do
    [Than] wishest should be undone.

6   High thee hither,
    That I may pour my spirits in thine ear,
    And chastise with the valor of my tongue
    All that impedes thee from the golden round,
    Which fate and metaphysical aid doth seem
    To have thee crown'd withal.

Lady

1   [Glamys] thou art, and Cawdor, and shalt be
     What thou art promis'd: yet doe I feare thy Nature,
     It is too full o'th'Milke of [humane] kindnesse,
     To catch the neerest way.

2   Thou would'st be great,
     Art not without Ambition, but without
     The illnesse should attend it.

3   What thou would'st highly,
     That would'st thou holily: would'st not play false,
     And yet would'st wrongly winne.

4   Thould'st have, great [Glamys], that which cryes,
     Thus thou must doe, if thou have it;
     And that which rather thou do'st feare to doe,
     [Then] wishest should be undone.

5   High thee hither,
     That I may powre my Spirits in thine Eare,
     And chastise with the valour of my Tongue
     All that impeides thee from the Golden Round,
     Which Fate and Metaphysicall ayde doth seeme
     To have thee crown'd withall.

• the speech starts very carefully, the opening intellectual surround phrase

> " . Glamys thou art, and Cawdor, and shalt be/What thou art promis'd : "

not simply summing up all that she knows to date but promising that the Weyward Sisters' prophecy will be fulfilled in full

• but her concerns that his nature is 'too full o'th'Milke of humane kindnesse' are very emotional (2/6, F #1's last two lines), which turns to passion as she so quickly assesses his fundamental flaw - that he want greatness but is not sufficiently ruthless to achieve it (F #2. 1/1)

• her further detailing of what she perceives as his weakness now becomes emotional (F #3-4, 1/6), and is immediately thrown into even greater relief with F #3's two surround phrases

> " . What thou would'st highly,/would'st thou holily : would'st not play false,/And yet would'st wrongly winne . "

• her F #4 understanding that her manipulative strength will lie in the fact that though he hears 'that which cryes,/Thus thou must doe, if thou have it ;' and fears it, he'd rather hear it 'Then wishest should be undone.' is underscored by

a/ the moment of realisation linking the two ideas, via the only emotional semicolon in the speech

b/ F #3's recognition of his weakness, marked by F's three irregular shaded lines (six/seven or eight/eight syllables) that suggest a pause before she begins to discover F #4's solution – a pause most modern texts remove by resetting the text as two almost pentameter lines (nine or ten/eleven), as shown

• at last, as she realises how she may manipulate him, passions spring forth (F #5, 7/8) as she envisages stirring him by pouring 'my Spirits in thine Eare'

The Tragedie of Macbeth

Lady Macbeth/Lady

The Raven himselfe is hoarse,
1.5.42 - 58

Background: In this speech, following the news that both Macbeth and the current king, Duncan, will arrive at the castle that same day, she appeals to the darker supernatural powers for help.

Style: solo

Where: somewhere in the castle at Inverness, possibly her private chambers

To Whom: self

# of Lines: 22

Probable Timing: 1.10 minutes

Take Note: With only one major piece of punctuation and no surround phrases it would seem that once she starts, rather than controlling the event, her recognition of what happens to her and her need to complete the transformation is what drives the speech - though the onrush after Macbeth's arrival may suggest that she cannot yet control the new being she has become.

Lady

1   The raven himself is hoarse
     That croaks the fatal entrance of Duncan
     Under my battlements.

2   Come, you spirits,
     That tend on mortal thoughts, unsex me here,
     And fill me from the crown to the toe top-full
     Of direst cruelty !

3   Make thick my blood,
     Stop up th'access and passage to remorse,
     That no compunctious visitings of nature
     Shake my fell purpose, nor keep peace between
     Th'effect, and [it] !

4   Come to my woman's breasts,
     Andtakemy milk for gall, you[murd'ring] ministers,
     Whereever in your sightless substances
     You wait on nature's mischief !

5   Come, thick night,
     And pall thee in the dunnest smoke of hell,
     That my keen knife see not the wound it makes,
     Nor heaven peep through the blanket of the dark
     To cry, hold, hold.

           [**Enter Macbeth**]

6   Great [Glamis] !, worthy Cawdor !
     Greater [than]both, by the all-hail hereafter !

7   Thy letters have transported me beyond
     This ignorant present, and I feel now
     The future in the instant.

Lady

1   The Raven himselfe is hoarse,
     That croakes the fatall entrance of Duncan
     Under my Battlements.

2   Come you Spirits,
     That tend on mortall thoughts, unsex me here,
     And fill me from the Crowne to the Toe, ₓ top-full
     Of direst Crueltie: make thick my blood,
     Stop up th'accesse, and passage to Remorse,
     That no compunctious visitings of Nature
     Shake my fell purpose, nor keepe peace betweene
     Th'effect, and [hit].

3   Come to my Womans Brests,
     AndtakemyMilkefor Gall, you [murth'ring] Ministers,
     Where-ever, in your sightlesse substances,
     You wait on Natures Mischiefe.

4   Come thick Night,
     And pall thee in the dunnest smoake of Hell,
     That my keene Knife see not the Wound it makes,
     Nor Heaven peepe through the Blanket of the darke,
     To cry, hold, hold.

               [Enter Macbeth]

5   Great [Glamys], worthy Cawdor,
     Greater [then] both, by the all-haile hereafter,
     Thy Letters have transported me beyond
     This ignorant present, and I feele now
     The future in the instant.

- whether real or symbolic, the opening recognition of the cry of the bird of foreboding (itself a fascinating contrast to the innocent and abundant 'temple-haunting martlet' that greeted Duncan and the royal party when they arrived) is voiced passionately (F #1, 3/3), while the first invitation to the 'Spirits/That tend on mortall thoughts' to 'unsex me' (4/2, F #2's first three lines) becomes more controlled

- but then the first of two onrushed moments in the speech mark what most modern texts regard as a slight loss of grammatical control (setting a more rational mt. #3), while the ensuing text turns passionate (2/3, the last four lines of F #2) - the two factors suggesting that perhaps the 'make thick my blood', and why, is a reaction to what is happening to her rather than an order to continue

- she seems to re-establish control of self and situation with F #3's 'Come to my Womans Brests' (7/3), and, to a lesser extent, in the double request for 'thick Night' to come, so she will not see 'the Wound' her knife makes, and 'Heaven' will not witness the attack on Duncan (F #4, 6/4)

- it may be more of a struggle for her to maintain such control than the modern texts suggest, for F has added four extra breath-thoughts, two in F #2 and one each in F #3-4, suggesting that what follows is of great difficulty for her to endure (', top-full/Of direst Crueltie'; ', and passage to Remorse,'), or is very specific to her needs (', in your sightlesse substances'; ', To cry, hold, hold')

- though most modern texts separate the greeting (mt. #6) and her description of the effect that his letter has had on her (mt. #7), F jams both together, this onrush suggesting a slight loss of control once more as he appears - again, as with the end of mt. #2, the content of the onrush is passionate (3/2)

The Tragedie of Macbeth

Lady Macbeth/Lady

What Beast was't {†}/That made you breake this enterprize to me?

between 1.7.47 - 72

Background: Having realised there is no legitimate or honest reason for killing Duncan, Macbeth informs his wife 'we will proceed no further in this Businesse'. These two speeches comprise the bulk of her eventually successful rhetoric which keeps him to the proposed task in hand, for he eventually responds not just with the admiring 'Bring forth Men-Children onely', but 'I am settled, and bend up/ Each corporall Agent to this terrible Feat'.

Style: as part of a two-handed scene

Where: Inverness castle, somewhere close to the ongoing banquet

To Whom: Macbeth

# of Lines: 26

Probable Timing: 1.15 minutes

Take Note: This comes from one of the trickiest sequences facing any actress in the whole of Shakespeare – for the temptation is to play it as an emotional attack from the outset, whereas F's opening establishes a struggle to maintain control, as if she were trying to avoid unnecessarily antagonising him, unless she has to.

Lady Macbeth

1   What beast was't {†}
    That made you break this enterprise to me?

2   When you durst do it, then you were a man;
    And to be more [than]what you were, you would
    Be so much more the man.

3   Nor time, nor place,
    Did then adhere, and yet you would make both:
    They have made themselves, and that their fitness now
    Do's unmake you.

4   I have given suck, and know
    How tender 'tis to love the babe that milks me;
    I would, while it was smiling in my face,
    Have pluck'd my nipple from his boneless gums,
    And dash'd the brains out, had I so sworn as you
    Have done to this.

---

5   {†} {S}crew your courage to the sticking place,
    And we'll not fail.

6   When Duncan is asleep
    (Whereto the rather shall his days hard journey
    Soundly invite him), his two chamberlains
    Will I with wine, and wassail so convince,
    That memory, the warder of the brain,
    Shall be a fume, and the receipt of reason
    A limbeck only.

7   When in swinish sleep
    Their drenched natures lies as in a death,
    What cannot you and I perform upon
    Th'unguarded Duncan? what not put upon
    His spungy officers, who shall bear the guilt
    Of our great quell?

Lady

1   What Beast was't {††}
     That made you breake this enterprize to me?

2   When you durst do it, then you were a man:
     And to be more [then] what you were, you would
     Be so much more the man.

3   Nor time, nor place
     Did then adhere, and yet you would make both:
     They have made themselves, and that their fitnesse now
     Do's unmake you.

4   I have given Sucke, and know
     How tender 'tis to love the Babe that milkes me,
     I would, while it was smyling in my Face,
     Have pluckt my Nipple from his Bonelesse Gummes,
     And dasht the Braines out, had I so sworne
     As you have done to this.

5   {††} {S}crew your courage to the sticking place,
     And wee'le not fayle: when Duncan is asleepe,
     (Whereto the rather shall his dayes hard Journey
     Soundly invite him) his two Chamberlaines
     Will I with Wine, and Wassell, so convince,
     That Memorie, the Warder of the Braine,
     Shall be a Fume, and the Receit of Reason
     A Lymbeck onely: when in Swinish sleepe,
     Their drenched Natures lyes as in a Death,
     What cannot you and I performe upon
     Th'unguarded Duncan?

6   What not put upon
     His spungie Officers? who shall beare the guilt
     Of our great quell.

• the speech opens very carefully, for after F #1's single striking capital release 'Beast' (building on her previous image of comparing Macbeth to the 'poore Cat i'th'Addage' and thus less than a man, an appallingly demeaning insult to any Elizabethan) and cunning emotional release 'enterprize' (suggesting that their acsending to the throne – by whatever means – is merely a business proposition)

• the care with which she is trying to win him by rational argument rather than off-putting emotion can be clearly seen in F #2 and nearly all of F #3's apparently reasonable debate, which is couched in three unembellished surround phrases (and monosyllabic save for the word 'adhere',)

> " . When you durst do it, then you were a man : And to be more then what you were, you would/Be so much more the man . Nor time, nor place/Did then adhere, and yet you would make both : / . . . "

• this control does not last, for the end of F #3 (the time's 'fitnesse') first plunges her into passion as she proves her valour to shame him into action (7/7, F #4), and then, in attempting to forestall his fear of failure (0/2, F #5's opening surround phrase 'Screw your courage to the sticking place/And wee'le not fayle') she momentarily becomes emotional

• that the full planning of the details excites her can be seen in her sudden enormous onrushed release (16/9, F #5's last nine lines), though whether the passion stems from the idea itself or in trying to get Macbeth to see and grasp the possibilities is up to each actor to explore: this onrush is removed by most modern texts setting two more rational sentences - mt. #6 for why Duncan will sleep, mt. #7 what they can then do to him

• indeed most modern texts regard F's final sentence as ungrammatical: as set F seems to suggest that at the very last moment her control slips just a little, yet the immediacy of the circumstances and the urgency of her final F #6 extra sentence demand ' . What not put upon/His spungie Officers ? who shall beare the guilt/Of our great quell . ' is underscored

a/ by being set as two surround phrases

b/ by the question mark acting as a link (here functioning as the modern exclamation mark)

c/ the slight emotion involved (1/2)

much more so than by the new modern rationality

The Tragedie of Macbeth
Lady Macbeth/Lady

Yet heere's a spot .
between 5.1.31 - 68

Background: Lady Macbeth is sick. She has been walking and talking in her sleep repeatedly, leaving no doubt as to her complicity in and/ or knowledge of the various murders that have enabled Macbeth to become, and then maintain his position as, King. Here she walks once more, not knowing that she is being closely watched by the Doctor and the Gentlewoman who has summoned him.

Style: solo, observed by two hidden watchers

Where: the castle at Dunsinane

To Whom: self, and the imagined presence of Macbeth

# of Lines: 17

Probable Timing: 0.55 minutes

Take Note: The large number of major punctuation marks (thirteen, of which only one is emotional), and the pronounced and quick switches between four different patterns of release underscore the Doctor's earlier description of her as being 'troubled with thicke-comming Fancies/That keepe her from her rest.' – for here her mind never stays on one topic or remains in one particular style for more than a brief moment.

Lady
1   Yet here's a spot.

2   Out, damned spot! out, I say!
3   One - two - why
    then 'tis time to do't.
4   Hell is murky.
5   Fie, my Lord, fie,
    a soldier, and afear'd?
6   What need we fear who knows
    it, when none can call our pow'r to accompt?

7   Yet who
    would have thought the old man to have had so much
    blood in him?

8   The Thane of Fife, had a wife; where is she now?
9   What, will these hands ne'er be clean?
10   No more o'that
    my lord, no more o'that; you mar all with this star-
    ting.

11 Here's the smell of the blood still.
12   All the per-
    fumes of Arabia will not sweeten this little hand.
13 O, O, O!

14 Wash your hands, put on your night-gown,
    look not so pale.
15   I tell you yet again, Banquo's buried;
    he cannot come out on's grave.

16 To bed, to bed; there's knocking at the gate.
17 Come, come, come, come, give me your hand.
18   What's
    done cannot be undone.
19   To bed, to bed, to bed.

Lady

1　Yet heere's a spot.

2　Out damned spot: out I say.
3　　　　　　　　　　　　　One: Two: Why
　　then 'tis time to doo't: Hell is murky.
4　　　　　　　　　　　　　Fye, my Lord, fie,
　　a Souldier, and affear'd? what need we feare? who knowes
　　it, when none can call our powre to accompt: yet who
　　would have thought the olde man to have had so much
　　blood in him.

5　The Thane of Fife, had a wife: where is she now?
6　What will these hands ne're be cleane?
7　　　　　　　　　　　　　No more o'that
　　my Lord, no more o'that: you marre all with this star-
　　ting.

8　Heere's the smell of the blood still: all the per-
　　fumes of Arabia will not sweeten this little hand.
9　Oh, oh, oh.

10　Wash your hands, put on your Night-Gowne,
　　looke not so pale: I tell you yet againe Banquo's buried;
　　he cannot come out on's grave.

11　To bed, to bed: there's knocking at the gate:
　　Come, come, come, come, give me your hand: What's
　　done, cannot be undone.
12　　　　　　　　　　　　To bed, to bed, to bed.

• the factual recollections and sometimes their current consequences - F #2 (her attempt to wash the blood off her hands); F #3 (the sound of the all-clear bell to summon them to kill Duncan); F #5 (the recollection of the now murdered Macduffe's wife); #F 7 (the attempt to keep Macbeth from becoming distracted by guilt from their plan); F #8, (the scent of the blood); F #10 (again instructions to Macbeth); F #11 (avoiding discovery by the arrival of Lenox and Macduffe) – are all heightened by being set as surround phrase sentences, as if each recollection is so disturbing as to give her pain – almost as if she were struggling to control each new memory so as not to be swamped by it

• the most disturbing of all the recollections seems to be F #10's last two emotional surround phrases

> " : I tell you yet againe Banquo's buried ; he cannot come out on's grave. "

since they are heightened by being linked by the only semicolon in the speech

• F's occasional onrush, where the juxtaposing of two ungrammatically connected ideas are joined in one sentence, shows where she is almost swamped - especially F #4's chastising of Macbeth plus the amount of blood spilled when Duncan was killed; F #10's ordering Macbeth to tidy himself plus the fact that Banquo cannot rise out of his grave; and F #11's repeated instructions 'to bed' plus 'What's done, cannot be undone'

• the unembellished monosyllabic surround phrases of F #2, ' . Out damned spot : out I say . ', suggest a moment of great determination in her attempt to rid herself of what she must feel would be the only evidence of their crime, while the calm of the almost completely unembellished finale

> "To bed, to bed : there's knocking at the gate : Come, come, come, come, give me your hand : What's done, cannot be undone . To bed, to bed, to bed ."

could well suggest that with all she has gone through her energy has at last drained away

The Tragedie of King Lear

Gonerill

Did my Father strike my Gentleman for chiding of his Foole?
between 1.3.1 - 26

Background: as was made clear at the end of the first scene where Lear divested himself of his powers as he divided up his kingdom, Gonerill and Regan are worried about Lear's possible behaviours as he stays with them, carefully referring to the difficulties that might be created by 'the infirmity of his age': Gonerill is the first to find how prescient her fears were

Style: as part of a two-handed scene

Where: the palace of Gonerill and Albany

To Whom: her Steward and right-hand man, Oswald

# of Lines: 18

Probable Timing: 0.55 minutes

Take Note: Q/F open with either prose or a long (15 syllable) verse line allowing Gonerill's unchecked intelligent indignation (3/1) to break all metric niceties; most modern texts amend the text in an attempt to control herself with hesitations of two short verse lines (9/6 syllables), presenting a much more controlled lady than was originally set.

Gonerill

1   Did my father strike my gentleman
     For chiding of his fool?

---

2   By day and night, he wrongs me, every hour
     He flashes into one gross crime or other
     That sets us all at odds.

3   I'll not endure it .

4   His knights grow riotous, and himself upbraids us
     On every trifle.

5   When he returns from hunting,
     I will not speak with him, say I am sick .

6   If you come slack of former services,
     You shall do well ; the fault of it I'll answer.

---

7   Put on what weary negligence you please,
     You and your fellows; I'd have it come to question .

8   If he distaste it, let him to my sister,
     Whose mind and mine I know in that are one,

9   Remember what I have said .

---

10   And let his knights have colder looks among you;
     What grows of it, no matter .

11   Advise your fellows so .

12   I'll write straight to my sister to hold my [very] course.

13   Prepare for dinner.

Gonerill

1   Did my Father strike my Gentleman for chiding of his Foole?

2   By day and night, he wrongs me, every howre
He flashes into one grosse crime, or other,
That sets us all at ods: Ile not endure it;
His Knights grow riotous, and himselfe upbraides us
On every trifle.
       ₃   When he returnes from hunting,
I will not speake with him, say I am sicke,
If you come slacke of former services,
You shall do well, the fault of it Ile answer.

4   Put on what weary negligence you please,
You and your Fellowes: I'de have it come to question;
If he distaste it, let him to my Sister,
Whose mind and mine I know in that are one,
Remember what I have said.

5   And let his Knights have colder lookes among
you: what growes of it no matter, advise your fellowes
so, Ile write straight to my Sister to hold my[] course; prepare for dinner.

• while at first glance her F #2 (1/4) decision to do something about her father's excesses should be emotional, the fact it is finally voiced as two determined but emotional surround phrases (linked by the first of three such semicolons scattered throughout the speech)

> " : Ile not endure it ; /His Knights grow riotous, and himselfe up-braides us/On every trifle . "

suggests perhaps it is not as easy for her to move against her father as some actresses/productions portray

• as she puts the plan into action (F #3) she continues emotionally (0/4), yet the possibility of who should take the blame is voiced very quietly

> "You shall do well, the fault of it Ile answer'

the unembellishment perhaps suggesting that in facing the enormity of what she is about to do she needs to calm both herself and her Steward

• this calmness in turn yields more determined (2/1) surround phrases

> " . Put on what weary negligence you please,/You and your Fellowes : I'de have it come to question ; "

the idea of forcing the issue heightened by the second emotional semicolon

• which apart from the one word 'Sister' (the key word relating to her fellow conspirator in the overall scheme) leads to the three line unembellished

> " . If he distaste it, let him to my Sister,/Whose mind and mine I know in that are one,/Remember what I have said . "

the quiet once more suggesting the determined need for calming

• the final instruction to 'let his Knights have colder lookes among you' while she writes to her Sister is passionate (2/3), and it seems she realises the forthcoming awkwardness will start once her final instruction ' ; prepare for dinner . ' is given, for it is surprisingly set as yet another emotional surround phrase – (perhaps she is somewhat disturbed by what she is putting into action)

The Tragedie of King Lear

Gonerill

Not only Sir this, your all-lycenc'd Foole,
between 1.4.201 - 222

Background: the Foole has just seen Lear almost play the inferior
to a (oft-)frowning Gonerill: pulling no punches, he has told Lear
to Gonerill's face 'Thou was't a pretty fellow when thou hadst no
need to care for her frowning . . . I am better than thou art now, I
am a Foole, thou art nothing': Gonerill, now begins to do what she
promised in her previous speech, pushing matters to a head because
she'll 'not endure it':

Style: public address

Where: her palace

To Whom: Lear, in front of the Foole, Kent/Caius and Lear's
attendants

# of Lines: 18

Probable Timing: 0.55 minutes

Take Note: As with the previous speech her calm is difficult to maintain, as the sudden orthographical outburst of F #3 (and the struggles through the remainder of the speech to re-establish public
composure) shows.

Gonerill

1   Not only, sir, this, your all-licens'd Fool,
    But other of your insolent retinue
    Do hourly carp and quarrel, breaking forth
    In rank, and not-to-be endur'd riots.

2   Sir,
    I had thought, by making this well known unto you,
    To have found a safe redress, but now grow fearful,
    By what yourself too late have spoke and done,
    That you protect this course and put it on
    By your allowance ; which if you should, the fault
    Would not scape censure, nor the redresses sleep,
    Which, in the tender of a wholesome weal,
    Might in their working do you that offense,
    Which else were shame, that [than] necessity
    Will call discreet proceeding.

---

3   I would you would make use of your good wisdom
    (Whereof I know you are fraught) and put away
    These dispositions which of late transport you
    From what you rightly are.

Gonerill

1　Not only Sir this, your all-lycenc'd Foole,
　　But other of your insolent retinue
　　Do hourely Carpe and Quarrell, breaking forth
　　In ranke, and (not to be endur'd) riots Sir.

2　I had thought by making this well knowne unto you,
　　To have found a safe redresse, but now grow fearefull
　　By what your selfe too late have spoke and done,
　　That you protect this course, and put it on
　　By your allowance, which if you should, the fault
　　Would not scape censure, nor the redresses sleepe,
　　Which in the tender of a wholesome weale,
　　Might in their working do you that offence,
　　Which else were shame, that [then] necessitie
　　Will call discreet proceeding.

3　I would you would make use of your good wisedome
　　(Whereof I know you are fraught), and put away
　　These dispositions, which of late transport you
　　From what you rightly are.

• by ending F #1's blunt passion remonstrance of the riotous behaviour of both the Foole and Lear's retinue with 'Sir.' followed by a period, Gonerill has repeated 'Sir' twice in one sentence, not a normal occurrence for someone in self-control: (Q sets a comma before 'Sir' and no punctuation after, still suggesting a character not in full control: most modern texts start F #2 before 'Sir', and set a comma after – thus showing much more verbal dignity for her than originally intended)

• then as she rather long-windedly, even awkwardly, explains how she had hoped her earlier mentioning of this would have rectified matters, all pretence to any intellectual self-control disappears, for her struggles to maintain dignity via five unembellished lines set in two different F #2 series -

> "That you protect this course, and put it on/By your allowance, which if you should, the fault/Would not scape censure,"

> "Might in their working do you that offence,/Which else were shame, that then necessitie/Will call discreet proceeding ."

is blown apart by her emotions (0/6, F #2's other four and a half lines)

• but it eventually seems her attempt at dignity succeeds, for F #3's final three and a half line rebuke/appeal for him to put away 'These dispositions' is unembellished save for the one keyword, as she appeals to his 'wisedome', though the two extra breath-thoughts show that it is a struggle for her to maintain composure

The Tragedie of King Lear

Gonerill

I would you would make use of your good wisedome
between 1.4.219 - 252

Background: continuing on the previous speech which dealt with the problem in general, while this speech proposes some unpleasant remedies

Style: public address

Where: her palace

To Whom: Lear, in front of the Foole, Kent/Caius and Lear's attendants

# of Lines: 18

Probable Timing: 0.55 minutes

Take Note: As with the previous speech her calm is difficult to maintain, as the sudden orthographical outburst of F #3 (and the struggles through the remainder of the speech to re-establish public composure) shows.

Gonerill

1   I would you would make use of your good wisdom
    (Whereof I know you are fraught) and put away
    These dispositions which of late transport you
    From what you rightly are.

    ---

2   I do beseech you
    To understand my purposes aright,
    As you are old and reverend, should be wise.

3   Here do you keep a hundred knights and squires,
    Men so disorder'd, so debosh'd and bold,
    That this our court, infected with their manners,
    Shows like a riotous inn.

4   Epicurism and lust
    Makes it more like a tavern or a brothel
    [Than] a grac'd palace.

5   The shame itself doth speak
    For instant remedy.

6   Be then desir'd
    By her, that else will take the thing she begs,
    A little to disquantity your train,
    And the remainders that shall still depend,
    To be such men as may besort your age,
    Which know themselves and you.

Gonerill

1 I would you would make use of your good wisedome
   (Whereof I know you are fraught), and put away
   These dispositions, which of late transport you
   From what you rightly are.

---

2   I do beseech you
   To understand my purposes aright:
   As you are Old, and Reverend, should be Wise.

3 Heere do you keepe a hundred Knights and Squires,
   Men so disorder'd, so debosh'd, and bold,
   That this our Court infected with their manners,
   Shewes like a riotous Inne;   Epicurisme and Lust
   Makes it more like a Taverne, or a Brothell,
   [Then] a grac'd Pallace.

4   The shame it selfe doth speake
   For instant remedy.

5   Be then desir'd
   By her, that else will take the thing she begges,
   A little to disquantity your Traine,
   And the remainders that shall still depend,
   To be such men as may besort your Age,
   Which know themselves, and you.

- starting where the previous speech left off, and repeating the last sentence, the three and a half line rebuke/appeal for Lear to put away 'These dispositions' is unembellished save for the one keyword, as she appeals to his 'wisedome', though the two extra breath-thoughts show that it is a struggle for her to maintain composure

- but F #2 opens with the very determined unembellished surround phrase

" . I do beseech you/To understand my purposes aright : "

which leads to the unequivocal intellectual demand to be 'Wise' (3/0), which would be fine if she could remain in such control, but she can't

- for F #3's onrushed listing of complaints bursts the bubble of her dignity, (9/7 in five and half lines), the only semicolon of the speech underscoring the emotional disgust/contempt/loathing in her 'Taverne . . . Brothell' rather than a 'grac'd Pallace' comparison, the whole a less controlled attack than the two more reasoned sentences used by her modern counterpart

- and emotion is all for her short F #4 'instant remedy' demand (0/2), and for her threat that Lear 'disquantity your Traine' or she 'will take the thing she begges' (0/2, F #5's first two and a half lines)

- then her appearance of dignity is captured once more as F #5's final three line demand that Lear retain only men of a certain 'Age', is unembellished, save for the pertinent word 'Age'

"And the remainders that shall still depend,/To be such men as may besort your Age,/Which know themselves, and you."

though whether the calm is genuine or enforced is up to each actor to explore

The Tragedie of King Lear
Cordelia

Alacke, 'tis he : why he was met even now
between 4.4.1 - 20

Background: learning of her father's treatment by her sisters, his current condition, and the threatened civil war between Albany and Cornwall, Cordelia has lead a troop of French forces to rectify the situation for both family and country: this is the first speech assigned her after landing

Style: address to a small group in front of a larger one

Where: the French encampment near Dover

To Whom: a small group of Gentlemen in front of soldiers

# of Lines: 16

Probable Timing: 0.50 minutes

Take Note: That the surround phrase ' . Alacke, tis he : 'opens the speech suggesst just how much Cordelia has hoped for the discovery of her father's whereabouts: the fact that of six surround phrases it is the only non-emotional one in the speech, and that orthographically the finish of the speech is highly emotional (1/6 the last three and half lines) shows just what effect the long sought for news has on her.

Cordelia

1　Alack, 'tis he !

2　　　　　　　　　　Why, he was met even now
　As mad as the vex'd sea, singing aloud,
　Crown'd with rank [femiter], and furrow-weeds,
　With [hardocks], hemlock, nettles, cuckoo-flowers,
　Darnel, and all the idle weeds that grow
　In our sustaining corn.

3　　　　　　　　　　　　A [century] send forth;
　Search every acre in the high-grown field,
　And bring him to our eye.

4　　What can man's wisdom
　In the restoring his bereaved sense ?

5　He that helps him, take all my outward worth.

6　All blest secrets,
　All you unpublish'd virtues of the earth
　Spring with my tears;　be aidant, and remediate
　In the good man's [distress] !

7　　　　　　　　　　　Seek, seek for him,
　Least his ungovern'd rage dissolve the life
　That wants the means to lead it.

Cordelia

1   Alacke, 'tis he: why he was met even now
As mad as the vext Sea, singing alowd,
  Crown'd with ranke [Fenitar], and furrow weeds,
With [Hardokes], Hemlocke, Nettles, Cuckoo flowres,
Darnell, and all the idle weedes that grow
In our sustaining Corne.

2   A [Centery] send forth;
Search every Acre in the high-growne field,
And bring him to our eye.

3   What can mans wisedome
In the restoring his bereaved Sense; he that helpes him,
Take all my outward worth.

---

4   All blest Secrets,
All you unpublish'd Vertues of the earth
  Spring with my teares; be aydant, and remediate
In the Goodmans [desires]: seeke, seeke for him,
Least his ungovern'd rage, dissolve the life
That wants the meanes to leade it.

- thus now knowing his general whereabouts, the order to search for him (F #2) and the promise to reward handsomely anyone who can cure him (F #3) while passionate (3/3) are set as four successive emotional surround phrases

  " . A Centery send forth ; /Search every Acre in the high-growne field,/And bring him to our eye . What can mans wisedome/In the restoring his bereaved Sense ; he that helpes him,/Take all my outward worth . "

- also emotional is the climax to her F #4 prayer to the 'Vertues of the earth'

  " ; be aydant, and remdiate/In the Goodmans [desires/distress] : '

- as the speech opens, the facts of her flower-crowned father are passionate (F 1, 7/6)

- as described above, the surround phrase orders to find him and offer of a reward to anyone who can cure him are passionate (3/3)

- and, for the only moment in the speech, in beginning her F #4 prayer, the naming to whom she is appealing, the 'blest Secrets' and 'Vertues of the earth', she is intellectually focused (2/0, the first line and a half) – but as she voices her request and then urges her followers to find her father before his 'rage, dissolve the life', intellect virtually disappears and she becomes highly emotional (1/6)

The Tragedie of King Lear
Cordelia

O my deere Father, restauration hang
between 4.7.25 - 43

Background: Cordelia's men have finally found her father, and in his maddened state have brought Lear back to camp in an effort to cure him: all medical preliminaries have been completed and now comes the dangerous and delicate moment when Lear has to be awoken to see whether the treatment has been successful or not

Style: one on one in front of a small supportive group

Where: the French encampment near Dover

To Whom: her father, in front of Kent, a Gentleman (sometimes referred to as 'Doctor') and servants who have carried Lear in

# of Lines: 16

Probable Timing: 0.50 minutes

Take Note: The fact of no major punctuation suggests this is essentially a stream of consciousness speech, each thought triggered by the one previous or Lear's appearance or (non-)reaction to what she's saying. One note, the shaded passage shown in the modern text comes from the quarto version of the play, and was not set in F.

Cordelia

1   O my dear father, restoration hang
    Thy medicine on my lips, and let this kiss
    Repair those violent harms that my two sisters
    Have in thy reverence made.

2   Had you not been their father, these white flakes
    Did challenge pity of them.

3   Was this a face
    To be oppos'd against the [warring] winds?
    [To stand against the deep dread-bolted thunder?
    In the most terrible and nimble stroke
    Of quick cross lightning? to watch - poor perdu ! -
    Within this thin helm?]

4   Mine enemy's dog,
    Though he had bit me, should have stood that night
    Against my fire, and wast thou fain (poor father)
    To hovel thee with swine and rogues forlorn
    In short and musty straw?

5   Alack, alack,
    'Tis wonder that thy life and wits at once
    Had not concluded all.

6   How does my royal lord?

7   How fares your Majesty

Cordelia

1   O my deere Father, restauration hang
    Thy medicine on my lippes, and let this kisse
    Repaire those violent harmes, that my two Sisters
    Have in thy Reverence made.

2   Had you not bin their Father, these white flakes
    Did challenge pitty of them.

3   Was this a face
    To be oppos'd against the [jarring] windes?
    [ ]

4   Mine Enemies dogge, though he had bit me,
    Should have stood that night against my fire,
    And was't thou faine (poore Father)
    To hovell thee with Swine and Rogues forlorne,
    In short, and musty straw?

5   Alacke, alacke,
    'Tis wonder that thy life and wits, at once
    Had not concluded all.

6   How does my Royall Lord?

7   How fares your Majesty?

- the only unembellished lines (the latter part of F #5) point to from where the impetus for her speech stems

    " 'Tis wonder that thy life and wits, at once/Had not concluded all . "

- Cordelia's opening wish that her kisses could be the medicine to cure the ravages her sisters have made on Lear's 'reverence' is emotional (F #1, 3/6)

- her wonder that anyone could harm such an old man (F #2), and throw him to the mercy of the winds (F #3), and make him 'hovell' with 'Swine and Rogues folorne', treating him worse that 'Mine Enemies dogge' (F #4) is expressed passionately (5/7)

- the precursor to the unembellished passage is emotional (0/2 the opening of F #5)

- and then, in questioning him directly (F #6-7) two things happen: first she becomes intellectual for the first time in the speech (2/1): second, the two short lines (5 or 6/6 syllables) setting for Cordelia allow an understandable hesitation between first and second questions: most modern texts follow Q and set a single line of verse, thus robbing her of the hesitation

The Tragedy of Coriolanus
Volumnia

I pray you daughter sing, or expresse your selfe
between 1.3.1 - 25

Background: Volumnia, Martius' mother, is a war-hawk, and proud of her son's accomplishments and reputation as a military killing machine; Virgilia, Martius' wife is the exact opposite: as they await news of the latest Roman war against Auffidius and the Volsces, the tension, and differences between them, are very apparent: speech #1 is a clear statement of Volumnia's personal philosophy

Style: as part of a two-handed scene, in front of a Gentlewoman

Where: Volumnia's home

To Whom: her daughter-in-law Virgilia

# of Lines: 21

Probable Timing: 1.10 minutes

Take Note; Volumnia's joy in her son and contempt of the softer aspects of life are clearly expressed in the language of the speech, and F's orthography seems to reveal just how (unhealthily) deep that joy lies.

Volumnia

1   I pray you daughter, sing, or express yourself
    in a more comfortable sort .

2   If my son were my hus-
    band, I should freelier rejoice in that absence wherein
    he won honor [than]in the embracements of his bed
    where he would show most love .

3   When yet he was but
    tender-bodied, and the only son of my womb ; when
    youth with comeliness pluck'd all gaze his way ; when
    for a day of kings' entreaties a mother should not sell him
    an hour from her beholding ; I, considering how honor
    would become such a person, that it was no better [than]
    picture-like to hang by th'wall, if renown made it not
    stir, was pleas'd to let him seek danger where he was
    like to find fame .

4   To a cruel war I sent him, from
    whence he return'd, his brows bound with oak .

5   I tell
    thee, Daughter, I sprang not more in joy at first hearing
    he was a man-child, [than] now in first seeing he had pro-
    v'd himself a man .

---

6   Hear me pro-
    fess sincerely : had I a dozen sons, each in my love alike,
    and none less dear [than] thine and my good Martius, I
    had rather had eleven die nobly for their country [than]
    one voluptuously surfeit out of action .

Volumnia

1   I pray you daughter sing, or expresse your selfe
in a more comfortable sort : If my Sonne were my Husband, I should freelier rejoyce in that absence wherein
he wonne Honor, [then] in the embracements of his Bed,
where he would shew most love.

2   When yet hee was but
tender-bodied, and the onely Sonne of my womb ; when
youth with comelinesse pluck'd all gaze his way ; when
for a day of Kings entreaties, a Mother should not sel him
an houre from her beholding ; I considering how Honour
would become such a person, that it was no better [then]
Picture-like to hang by th'wall, if renowne made it not
stirre, was pleas'd to let him seeke danger, where he was
like to finde fame : To a cruell Warre I sent him, from
whence he return'd, his browes bound with Oake.

3   I tell
thee Daughter, I sprang not more in joy at first hearing
he was a Man-child, [then] now in first seeing he had pro-
ved himselfe a man.

4   Heare me pro-
fesse sincerely, had I a dozen sons each in my love alike,
and none lesse deere [then] thine, and my good Martius, I
had rather had eleven dye Nobly for their Countrey, [then]
one voluptuously surfet out of Action.

- the emotional underpinnings to Volumnia's fixation on son Martius can be seen in F #2's emotional (semicolon created) surround phrases

   " . When yet hee was but tender-bodied, and the onely Sonne of my womb ; when youth with comelinesse pluck'd all gaze his way ; "

and her pride in him in the final surround phrase of the same sentence

   " : To a cruell Warre I sent him, from whence he return'd, his browes bound with Oake . "

- whatever Volumnia's emotional attitude (0/2) towards her daughter-in-law (scorn? impatience?), it is heightened by her first words of the speech being set as a surround phrase, and her belief in 'Honor' above all is is expressed intellectually (5/3, F #1's remaining three lines), while the extra breath-thoughts that suddenly appear could well point to her scorn of setting importance in the 'embracements of his Bed,', they could also mark her personal excitement in the joy of war and of her son in war

- Volumnia's setting up of when Martius was a youth though she as 'a Mother should not sel him an houre from her beholding' is passionate (3/4, F #2's first four lines); her extended belief 'how Honour' was nothing if 'renowne made it not stirre' (2/5, F #2's next four lines) is emotional; and her passions sweep in once more in expressing what this belief inevitably ensured, that, despite his youth, 'To a cruell Warre I sent him', (3/4 in just the last line and a half of F #2)

- Volumnia's F#3 comparing her joy of her son's proof of manhood through war to that of his birth is passionate, but more relaxed (2/1)

- and, as in F #1, though F 4's sudden and grammatically unnecessary extra breath-thoughts might simply show just how carefully Volumnia is pointing out to Virgilia the depth of her (sacrificial) patriotism, since so much of F #2 has been spent on the (excitement?) joy that Coriolanus brings her, this may be as revelatory of the depth of her need to live through him and his victories, as her beliefs – the whole being expressed in high passion once more (4/6 in just four lines)

The Tragedy of Coriolanus
Volumnia

Now it lyes you on to speake to th'people :
3.2.52 – 69

Background: it was his mother's ambition which caused Coriolanus to seek political office, and now Volumnia attempts to counsel her son as to what he must do to retrieve the situation: this speech, shows the wide gulf between her expectations and his, for to her the end justifies the means, lying and all

Style: one on one address in front of a small group

Where: Volumnia's home

To Whom: Coriolanus, in front of his supporting nobles, and Menenius and the more cautious Senators

# of Lines: 18

Probable Timing: 0.55 minutes

Take Note: F's orthography shows that while Volumnia may have difficulty in opening it seems she successfully manages to get back on intellectual track – only to lose control – whether deliberately or no – at the very last moment.

Volumnia

1   Now it lies [on you] to speak
To th'people ;   not by your own instruction,
Nor by th'matter which your heart prompts you,
But with such words that are but roted
In your tongue, though but bastards and syllables
Of no allowance, to your bosom's truth.

2   Now, this no more dishonors you at all
[Than] to take in a town with gentle words,
Which else would put you to your fortune and
The hazard of much blood.

3   I would dissemble with my nature where
My fortunes and my friends at stake requir'd
I should do so in honor.

4   I am in this
Your wife, your son , these senators, the nobles;
And you will rather show our general louts
How you can frown, [than] spend a fawn upon 'em
For the inheritance of their loves and safeguard
Of what that want might ruin.

Volumnia

1　Now it lyes [you on] to speake to th'people :
　Not by your owne instruction, nor by'th'matter
　Which your heart prompts you, but with such words
　That are but roated in your Tongue ;
　Though but Bastards, and Syllables
　Of no allowance, to your bosomes truth.

2　Now, this no more dishonors you at all,
　[Then] to take in a Towne with gentle words,
　Which else would put you to your fortune, and
　The hazard of much blood.

3　I would dissemble with my Nature, where
　My Fortunes and my Friends at stake, requir'd
　I should do so in Honor.

4　　　　　　　　　　　I am in this
　Your Wife, your Sonne : These Senators, the Nobles,
　And you, will rather shew our generall Lowts,
　How you can frowne, [then] spend a fawne upon 'em,
　For the inheritance of their loves, and safegard
　Of what that want might ruine.

• establishing the need for him to lie, and not be disconcerted by it since his words would be 'but Bastards, and Syllables of no allowance', she opens passionately (F #1, 4/4), though this may not be easy for her to put forward, for

a/ the kernel of her argument is expressed as an opening surround phrase

   " . Now it lyes on you to speake to th'people : "

b/ F #1's middle irregular four line structure (11/9/8/8 syllables as shaded) seems to suggest Volumnia carefully gathering herself before beginning this very tricky stage of the argument, and . . .

• . . . F #2's unembellished lines (save for the one word 'Towne', which points to the military comparison with which she is trying to draw a parallel), show her trying to head off any suggestion from Coriolanus that her advice may be dishonourable

   "Now, this no more dishonors you at all,/Then to take in a Towne with gentle words,/Which else would put you to your fortune, and/The hazard of much blood . "

• and having launched herself fully into attack-mode, her initial follow-up to the non-dishonourable argument, (that she would do anything for Friends in the name of 'Honor') is totally intellectual (4/0, F #3) - as is the first line and half of F #4's claim (5/1) that in this she is speaking for all that should be dear to him ('Wife', Sonne', 'These Senators', 'Nobles')

• but then her control shatters for as she accuses him of being unwilling to show the 'generall Lowts' anything other than a 'frowne', her passion spills over (4/4, F #4's last three and a half lines), though whether this is a deliberate ploy to shame him, or a genuine loss of control, is up to each actor to explore . . .

• . . . and the extra breath-thoughts that have been scattered throughout the speech suddenly gather together in this unexpected cluster of releases – though whether this is because she is trying to ensure every distasteful point is rammed home, or trying to prevent herself from losing control altogether is again up to each actor to explore

The Tragedie of
Anthonie and Cleopatra
Cleopatra

Oh Charmion :/Where think'st thou he is now ?
1.5.18 - 34

Background: with Anthony's return to Rome for military discussions, Cleopatra cannot keep him out of her mind: the speech is self-explanatory, the second part added from a speech coming somewhat later in Anthony's absence

Style: one on one address for the benefit of the rest of the small group

Where: Cleopatra's palace

To Whom: Charmian, Iras and the eunuch Mardian

# of Lines: 16

Probable Timing: 0.50 minutes

Take Note: Fs orthography shows how Cleopatra's thoughts of love, coloured by her concerns about her age, her (fading?) beauty and Anthony's absence, run the complete gamut from the opening brief moments of intellect and quietness through to emotion and passion, and not always where expected.

Cleopatra

1   O Charmian !
    Where think'st thou he is now ?

2   Stands he, or sits he ?

3   Or does he walk ?

4   Or is he on his horse ?

5   O happy horse, to bear the weight of Antony !

6   Do bravely, horse, for wot'st thou whom thou mov'st ?
    The demi-Atlas of this earth, the arm
    And burgonet of men.

7   He's speaking now,
    Or murmuring, "Where's my serpent of old Nile ?"
    (For so he calls me.)

8   Now I feed myself
    With most delicate poison.

9   Think on me,
    That am with Phœbus' amorous pinches black,
    And wrinkled deep in time ?

10   Broad-fronted Cæsar,
    When thou wast here above the ground, I was
    A morsel for a monarch;   and great Pompey
    Would stand and make his eyes grow in my brow;
    There would [he anchor his] aspect, and die
    With looking on his life.

Cleopatra

1   Oh Charmion:
    Where think'st thou he is now?

2   Stands he, or sits he?

3   Or does he walke?

4   Or is he on his Horse?

5   Oh happy horse to beare the weight of Anthony!

6   Do bravely Horse, for wot'st thou whom thou moov'st,
    The demy Atlas of this Earth, the Arme
    And Burganet of men.

7   Hee's speaking now,
    Or murmuring, where's my Serpent of old Nyle,
    (For so he cals me:) Now I feede my selfe
    With most delicate poyson.

8   Thinke on me
    That am with Phœbus amorous pinches blacke,
    And wrinkled deepe in time.

9   Broad-fronted Cæsar,
    When thou was't heere above the ground, I was
    A morsell for a Monarke: and great Pompey
    Would stand and make his eyes grow in my brow,
    There would [be anchor this] Aspect, and dye
    With looking on his life.

• in addition to the words/images themselves the intensity of Cleopatra's longing is underscored

   a/ by the shortness of the first five sentences

   b/ their mixture of unembellishment and passion (3/3)

   c/ F #1's first words heightened by being set as two surround phrases

   d/ apart from the name 'Charmion' the first four sentences are expressed as monosyllables

   e/ F #5 ends with a very rare (for Elizabethan/Jacobean texts) exclamation mark

• her speaking to the horse she imagines carrying Anthony, ordering it to 'Do bravely' since it is carrying 'The demy-Atlas of this Earth', is strongly released (slightly more intellectually than emotionally, 5/3, F #6's three lines)

• her imagining Anthony murmuring his desire for her is intellectual (3/1, the first two lines of F #8)

• then she becomes highly emotional as she realises via the surround phrase

   " : Now I feede my selfe/With most delicate poyson . "

   and calling out to him that he should think of her - even though she is not the - Elizabethan - concept of true beauty either in age or skin tone - (2/6, the last line of F #7 and all of F #8)

• and with the thoughts of love she recalls how she was worthily the focus of attention with her previous great partners, Cæsar and Pompey (F #9), and not surprisingly she becomes passionate once more (4/4)

The Tragedie of Anthonie and Cleopatra

Cleopatra

I dreampt there was an Emperor Anthony .

between 5.2.76 - 94

Background: conclusively beaten by Cæsar's forces, lied to (at
Cleopatra's insistence) and therefore believing Cleopatra is dead,
Anthony clumsily committed suicide and died a painful death: despite Cæsar's promises of friendship and respect, Cleopatra's private
quarters have been invaded by Roman forces, and she and her wom-
en are essentially prisoners: Dolabella, one of Cæsar's loyal support-
ers, one of many she was advised not to trust, has just joined her,
and she essentially has refused to acknowledge his opening greetings, challenging him instead with the rather oblique 'You laugh
when Boyes or Women tell their Dreames,/Is't not your tricke?'

Style: as part of a five-handed scene, initially directed to one man

Where: private quarters in Cleopatra's palace

To Whom: Dolabella, in front of Charmian, Iras, and the eunuch
Mardian

# of Lines: 18

Probable Timing: 0.55 minutes

Take Note: F #7's final emotional orthography (0/3) as she asks
Dolabella whether such a man as she has extolled could exist is
most surprising, and this is the crux of the speech – for if she is in
control throughout, it could be a direct challenge to Dolabella to
deny it if he dare, but if she has lost self-control, it could be she is
seeking help in deciding whether she has 'dreampt' all this, or no.

Background

Cleopatra

1 I dreamt there was an Emperor Antony.

2 O such another sleep, that I might see
   But such another man !

---

3 His face was as the heav'ns, and therein stuck
   A sun and moon, which kept their course, & lighted
   The little O, th'earth.

---

4 His legs bestrid the ocean, his rear'd arm
   Crested the world, his voice was propertied
   As all the tuned spheres, and that to friends;
   But when he meant to quail and shake the orb,
   He was as rattling thunder.

5   For his bounty,
   There was no winter in't; an [autumn t'was]
   That grew the more by reaping.

6   His delights
   Were dolphin-like, they show'd his back above
   The element they liv'd in.

7   In his livery
   Walk'd crowns and crownets; realms & islands were
   As plates dropp'd from his pocket.

---

8 Thinke you there was or might be such a man
   As this I dreamt of?

Cleopatra

1 I dreampt there was an Emperor Anthony.

2 Oh such another sleepe, that I might see
   But such another man.

---

3 His face was as the Heav'ns, and therein stucke
   A Sunne and Moone, which kept their course, & lighted
   The little o'th'earth.

---

4 His legges bestrid the Ocean, his rear'd arme
   Crested the world: His voyce was propertied
   As all the tuned Spheres, and that to Friends:
   But when he meant to quaile, and shake the Orbe,
   He was as ratling Thunder.

5   For his Bounty,
   There was no winter in't.

6   An [Anthony it was],
   That grew the more by reaping: His delights
   Were Dolphin-like, they shew'd his backe above
   The Element they liv'd in: In his Livery
   Walk'd Crownes and Crownets: Realms & Islands were
   As plates dropt from his pocket.

---

7 Thinke you there was, or might be such a man
   As this I dreampt of?

- the first thoughts of her now dead Anthony are passionate (5/6, the first four lines of the speech), the first two sentences, attesting to there will be no-one like him again, heightened by being short

- and F #3's hyperbole of the 'Sunne and Moone' were embodied in him 'which kept their course, & lighted/The little o'th'earth' finishes without embellishment, suggesting the magnificence of her dream and memories so triggered have quietened her down completely

- and in her F #4 painting of him as a super-being her passions flow back in (6/5), heightened by the two surround phrases

   " . His legges bestrid the Ocean, his rear'd arme/Crested the world : His voyce was propertied/As all the tuned Spheres, and that to Friends : "

- as she turns from his physical attributes to his generosity and influence on those around him (F #5-6), though the hyperbole continues she moves from passion to strong intellect in just six lines (11/2), as if these were more substantial memories (based on fact perhaps?)

- though most modern texts regard F #5 as ungrammatical, and add it to the information that follows, F Cleopatra's singling out Anthony's 'Bounty' being so generous it never ceased as a separate sentence points to just how fundamental a memory this is for her to cling onto

- and the fact F #6 is expressed as both onrushed and set as four consecutive surround phrases shows how deeply these memories are etched (and perhaps just how much need she has of them at this moment)

BIBLIOGRAPHY

AND

APPENDICES

The most easily accessible general information is to be found under the citations of *Campbell*, and of *Halliday*. The finest summation of matters academic is to be found within the all-encompassing *A Textual Companion*, listed below in the first part of the bibliography under *Wells, Stanley and Taylor, Gary* (eds.)

Individual modem editions consulted are listed below under the separate headings 'The Complete Works in Compendium Format' and 'The Complete Works in Separate Individual Volumes,' from which the modem text audition speeches have been collated and compiled.

All modem act, scene, and/or line numbers refer the reader to *The Riverside Shakespeare,* in my opinion still the best of the complete works, despite the excellent compendiums that have been published since.

The F/Q material is taken from a variety of already published sources, including not only all the texts listed in the 'Photostatted Reproductions in Compendium Format' below, but also earlier individually printed volumes, such as the twentieth century editions published under the collective title *The Facsimiles of Plays from The First Folio of Shakespeare* by Faber & Gwyer, and the nineteenth century editions published on behalf of The New Shakespere Society.

The heading 'Single Volumes of Special Interest' is offered to newcomers to Shakespeare in the hope that the books may add useful knowledge about the background and craft of this most fascinating of theatrical figures.

PHOTOSTATTED REPRODUCTIONS OF THE ORIGINAL TEXTS IN COMPENDIUM FORMAT

Allen, M.J.B. and K. Muir, (eds.). *Shakespeare's Plays in Quarto.* Berkeley: University of California Press, 1981.

Blaney, Peter (ed.). *The Norton Facsimile (The First Folio of Shakespeare).* New York: W.W.Norton & Co., Inc., 1996 (see also Hinman, below).

Brewer D.S. (ed.). *Mr. William Shakespeare's Comedies, Histories & Tragedies, The Second/Third/Fourth Folio Reproduced in Facsimile.* (3 vols.), 1983.

Hinman, Charlton (ed.). *The Norton Facsimile (The First Folio of Shakespeare)*. New York: W.W.Norton & Company, Inc., 1968.

Kokeritz, Helge (ed.). *Mr. William Shakespeare 's Comedies, Histories & Tragedies*. New Haven: Yale University Press, 1954.

Moston, Doug (ed.). *Mr. William Shakespeare's Comedies, Histories, and Tragedies*. New York: Routledge, 1998.

MODERN TYPE VERSION OF THE FIRST FOLIO IN COMPENDIUM FORMAT

Freeman, Neil. (ed.). *The Applause First Folio of Shakespeare in Modern Type*. New York & London: Applause Books, 2001.

MODERN TEXT VERSIONS OF THE COMPLETE WORKS IN COMPENDIUM FORMAT

Craig, H. and D. Bevington (eds.). *The Complete Works of Shakespeare*. Glenview: Scott, Foresman and Company, 1973.

Evans, G.B. (ed.). *The Riverside Shakespeare*. Boston: Houghton Mifflin Company, 1974.

Wells, Stanley and Gary Taylor (eds.). *The Oxford Shakespeare, William Shakespeare , the Complete Works, Original Spelling Edition,* Oxford: The Clarendon Press, 1986.

Wells, Stanley and Gary Taylor (eds.). *The Oxford Shakespeare, William Shakespeare, The Complete Works, Modern Spelling Edition*. Oxford: The Clarendon Press, 1986.

MODERN TEXT VERSIONS OF THE COMPLETE WORKS IN SEPARATE INDIVIDUAL VOLUMES

The Arden Shakespeare. London: Methuen & Co. Ltd., Various dates, editions, and editors .

Folio Texts. Freeman, Neil H. M. (ed.) Applause First Folio Editions, 1997, and following.

The New Cambridge Shakespeare. Cambridge: Cambridge University Press. Various dates, editions, and editors.

New Variorum Editions of Shakespeare. Furness, Horace Howard (original editor.). New York: 1880, Various reprints. All these volumes have been in a state of re-editing and reprinting since they first appeared in 1880. Various dates, editions, and editors.

The Oxford Shakespeare. Wells, Stanley (general editor). Oxford: Oxford University Press, Various dates and editors.

The New Penguin Shakespeare . Harmondsworth, Middlesex: Penguin Books, Various dates and editors.

The Shakespeare Globe Acting Edition. Tucker, Patrick and Holden, Michael. (eds.). London: M.H.Publications, Various dates.

SINGLE VOLUMES OF SPECIAL INTEREST

Baldwin, T.W. *William Shakespeare's Petty School.* 1943.

Baldwin, T.W. *William Shakespeare's Small wtin and Lesse Greeke.* (2 vols.) 1944.

Barton, John. *Playing Shakespeare.* 1984.

Beckerman, Bernard. *Shakespeare at the Globe, I 599-1609.* 1962. Berryman, John. *Berryman 's Shakespeare.* 1999.

Bloom, Harold. *Shakespeare: The Invention of the Human.* 1998. Booth, Stephen (ed.). *Shakespeare's Sonnets.* 1977.

Briggs, Katharine. *An Encyclopedia of Fairies.* 1976.

Campbell, Oscar James, and Edward G. Quinn (eds.). *The Reader's Encyclopedia of Shakespeare. 1966.*

Crystal, David, and Ben Crystal. *Shakespeare's Words: A Glossary & Language Companion.* 2002.

Flatter, Richard. *Shakespeare's Producing Hand.* 1948 (reprint).

Ford, Boris. (ed.). *The Age of Shakespeare.* 1955.

Freeman, Neil H.M. *Shakespeare's First Texts.* 1994.

Greg, W.W. *The Editorial Problem in Shakespeare: A Survey of the Foundations of the Text.* 1954 (3rd. edition).

Gurr, Andrew . *Playgoing in Shakespeare's London.* 1987. Gurr, Andrew. *The Shakespearean Stage, 1574-1642.* 1987. Halliday, F.E. *A Shakespeare Companion.* 1952.

Harbage, Alfred. *Shakespeare's Audience.* 1941.

Harrison, G.B. (ed.). *The Elizabethan Journals.* 1965 (revised, 2 vols.).

Harrison, G.B. (ed.). *A Jacobean Journal.* 1941.

Harrison, G.B. (ed.). *A Second Jacobean Journal.* 1958.

Hinman, Charlton. *The Printing and Proof Reading of the First Folio of Shakespeare.* 1963 (2 vols.).

Joseph, Bertram. *Acting Shakespeare.* 1960.

Joseph, Miriam (Sister). *Shakespeare's Use of The Arts of wnguage.*1947.

King, T.J. *Casting Shakespeare's Plays.* 1992.

Lee, Sidney and C.T. Onions. *Shakespeare's England : An Account Of The Life And Manners Of His Age.* (2 vols.) 1916.

Linklater, Kristin. *Freeing Shakespeare's Voice.* 1992.

Mahood, **M .M**. *Shakespeare's Wordplay.* 1957.

O'Connor, Gary. *William Shakespeare: A Popular Life.* 2000.

Ordish, T.F. *Early London Theatres.* 1894. (1971 reprint).

Rodenberg, Patsy. *Speaking Shakespeare.* 2002.

Schoenbaum. S. *William Shakespeare: A Documentary Life.* 1975.

Shapiro, Michael. *Children of the Revels.* 1977.

Simpson, Percy. *Shakespeare's Punctuation.* 1969 (reprint).

Smith, Irwin. *Shakespeare's Blackfriars Playhouse .* 1964.

Southern, Richard. *The Staging of Plays Before Shakespeare.* 1973.

Spevack, M. *A Complete and Systematic Concordance to the Works Of Shakespeare .* 1968-1980 (9vols.).

Tillyard, E.M.W. *The Elizabethan World Picture.* 1942.

Trevelyan, G.M. (ed.). *Illustrated English Social History.* 1942.

Vendler, Helen. *The Art of Shakespeare's Sonnets.* 1999.

Walker, Alice F. *Textual Problems of the First Folio.* 1953.

Walton, J.K. *The Quarto Copy of the First Folio.* 1971.

Warren, Michael. *William Shakespeare, The Parallel King Lear 1608-1623.*

Wells, Stanley and Taylor, Gary (eds.). *Modernising Shakespeare's Spelling, with Three Studies in The Text of Henry V.* 1975.

Wells, Stanley. *Re-Editing Shakespeare for the Modern Reader.* 1984.

Wells, Stanley and Gary Taylor (eds.). *William Shakespeare: A Textual Companion .* 1987.

Wright, George T. *Shakespeare's Metrical Art.* 1988.

HISTORICAL DOCUMENTS

Daniel, Samuel. *The Fowre Bookes of the Civile Warres Between The Howses Of Lancaster and Yorke.* 1595.

Holinshed, Raphael. *Chronicles of England, Scotland and Ireland.* 1587 (2nd. edition).

Halle, Edward. *The Union of the Two Noble and Illustre Famelies of Lancastre And Yorke.* 1548 (2nd. edition).

Henslowe, Philip: Foakes, R.A. and Rickert (eds.). *Henslowe's Diary.* 1961.

Plutarch: North, Sir Thomas (translation of a work in French prepared by Jacques Amyots). *The Lives of The Noble Grecians and Romanes.* 1579.

APPENDIX 1:
GUIDE TO THE EARLY TEXTS

A QUARTO (Q)

A single text, so called because of the book size resulting from a particular method of printing. Eighteen of Shakespeare's plays were published in this format by different publishers at various dates between 1594-1622, prior to the appearance of the 1623 Folio.

THE FIRST FOLIO (F1)'

Thirty-six of Shakespeare's plays (excluding *Pericles* and *Two Noble Kinsmen,* in which he had a hand) appeared in one volume, published in 1623. All books of this size were termed Folios, again because of the sheet size and printing method, hence this volume is referred to as the First Folio. For publishing details see Bibliography, 'Photostated Reproductions of the Original Texts.'

THE SECOND FOLIO (F2)

Scholars suggest that the Second Folio, dated 1632 but perhaps not published until 1640, has little authority, especially since it created hundreds of new problematic readings of its own. Nevertheless more than 800 modern text readings can be attributed to it. The **Third Folio** (1664) and the **Fourth Folio** (1685) have even less authority, and are rarely consulted except in cases of extreme difficulty.

APPENDIX 2:
WORD, WORDS, WORDS

PART ONE: VERBAL CONVENTIONS (AND HOW THEY WILL BE SET IN THE FOLIO TEXT)

"THEN" AND "THAN"

These two words, though their neutral vowels sound different to modern ears, were almost identical to Elizabethan speakers and readers, despite their different meanings. F and Q make little distinction between them, setting them interchangeably . The original setting will be used, and the modern reader should soon get used to substituting one for the other as necessary.

"I," "AY," AND "AYE"

F/Q often print the personal pronoun "I" and the word of agreement "aye" simply as "I." Again, the modern reader should quickly get used to this and make the substitution when necess ary. The reader should also be aware that very occasionally either word could be used and the phrase make perfect sense, even though different meanings would be implied.

"MY SELFE/HIM SELFE/HER SELFE" VERSUS "MYSELF/HIMSELF/HER-SELF"

Generally F/Q separate the two parts of the word, "my selfe" while most modern texts set the single word "myself." The difference is vital, based on Elizabethan philosophy. Elizabethans regarded themselves as composed of two parts, the corporeal "I," and the more spiritual part, the "self." Thus, when an Elizabethan character refers to "my selfe," he or she is often referring to what is to all intents and purposes a separate being, even if that being is a particular part of him- or herself. Thus soliloquies can be thought of as a debate between the "I" and "my selfe," and, in such speeches, even though there may be only one character on-stage, it's as if there were two distinct entities present.

UNUSUAL SPELLING OF REAL NAMES, BOTH OF PEOPLE AND PLACES

Real names, both of people and places, and foreign languages are often reworked for modern understanding. For example, the French town often set in Fl as "Callice" is usually reset as "Calais." F will be set as is.

NON-GRAMMATICAL USES OF VERBS IN BOTH TENSE AND APPLICATION

Modern texts 'correct' the occasional Elizabethan practice of setting a singular noun with plural verb (and vice versa), as well as the infrequent use of the past tense of a verb to describe a current situation. The F reading will be set as is, without annotation.

ALTERNATIVE SETTINGS OF A WORD WHERE DIFFERENT SPELLINGS MAINTAIN THE SAME MEANING

F/Q occasionally set what appears to modern eyes as an archaic spelling of a word for which there is a more common modern alternative, for example "murther" for murder , "burthen" for burden, "moe" for more, "vilde" for vile. Though some modern texts set the Fl (or alternative Q) setting, others modernise. Fl will be set as is with no annotation.

ALTERNATIVE SETTINGS OF A WORD WHERE DIFFERENT SPELLINGS SUGGEST DIFFERENT MEANINGS

Far more complicated is the situation where, while an Elizabethan could substitute one word formation for another and still imply the same thing, to modern eyes the substituted word has an entirely different meaning to the one it has replaced. The following is by no means an exclusive list of the more common dual-spelling, dual-meaning words

anticke-antique	mad-made	sprite-spirit
born-borne	metal-mettle	sun-sonne
hart-heart	mote-moth	travel-travaill
human-humane	pour-(po wre)-power	through-thorough
lest-least	reverent-reverend	troth-truth
lose-loose	right-rite	whether-whither

Some of these doubles offer a metrical problem too, for example "sprite," a one syllable word, versus "spirit." A potential problem occurs in *A Midsummer Nights Dream,* where the modern text s set Q1's "thorough," and thus the scansion pattern of elegant magic can be established, whereas F1's more plebeian "through" sets up a much more awkward and clumsy moment.

The F reading will be set in the Folio Text, as will the modern texts' substitution of a different word formation in the Modern Text. If the modern text substitution has the potential to alter the meaning (and sometimes scansion) of the line, it will be noted accordingly.

PART TWO: WORD FORMATIONS COUNTED AS EQUIVALENTS FOR THE FOLLOWING SPEECHES

Often the spelling differences between the original and modern texts are quite obvious, as with "she"/"shee". And sometimes Folio text passages are so flooded with longer (and sometimes shorter) spellings that, as described in the General Introduction, it would seem that vocally something unusual is taking place as the character speaks.

However, there are some words where the spelling differences are so marginal that they need not be explored any further. The following is by no means an exclusive list of words that in the main will not be taken into account when discussing emotional moments in the various commentaries accompanying the audition speeches.

(modern text spelling shown first)

and- &	murder - murther	tabor - taber
apparent - apparant	mutinous - mutenous	ta'en - tane
briars - briers	naught - nought	then - than
choice - choise	obey - obay	theater - theatre
defense - defence	o'er - o're	uncurrant - uncurrent
debtor - debter	offense - offence	than - then
enchant - inchant	quaint - queint	venomous - venemous
endurance - indurance	reside - recide	virtue - vertue
ere - e'er	Saint - S.	weight - waight
expense - expence	sense - sence	
has - ha's	sepulchre - sepulcher	
heinous - hainous	show - shew	
I'll - Ile	solicitor - soliciter	
increase - encrease	sugar - suger	

APPENDIX 3:
THE PATTERN OF MAGIC, RITUAL &
INCANTATION

THE PATTERNS OF "NORMAL" CONVERSATION

The normal pattern of a regular Shakespearean verse line is akin to five pairs of human heart beats, with ten syllables being arranged in five pairs of beats, each pair alternating a pattern of a weak stress followed by a strong stress. Thus, a normal ten syllable heartbeat line (with the emphasis on the capitalised words) would read as

weak- STRONG, weak - STRONG, weak- STRONG, weak- STRONG, weak- STRONG
(shall I com- PARE thee TO a SUMM- ers DAY)

Breaks would either be in length (under or over ten syllables) or in rhythm (any combinations of stresses other than the five pairs of weak-strong as shown above), or both together.

THE PATTERNS OF MAGIC, RITUAL, AND INCANTATION

Whenever magic is used in the Shakespeare plays the form of the spoken verse changes markedly in two ways . The length is usually reduced from ten to just seven syllables, and the pattern of stresses is completely reversed, as if the heartbeat was being forced either by the circumstances of the scene or by the need of the speaker to completely change direction. Thus in comparison to the normal line shown above, or even the occasional minor break, the more tortured and even dangerous magic or ritual line would read as

STRONG - weak, STRONG- weak, STRONG - weak, STRONG
(WHEN shall WE three MEET a GAINE)

The strain would be even more severely felt in an extended passage, as when the three weyward Sisters begin the potion that will fetch Macbeth to them. Again, the spoken emphasis is on the capitalised words and the effort of, and/or fixed determination in, speaking can clearly be felt.

> THRICE the BRINDed CAT hath MEW"D
> THRICE and ONCE the HEDGE-Pigge WHIN"D
> HARPier CRIES, 'tis TIME, 'tis TIME.

UNUSUAL ASPECTS OF MAGIC

It's not always easy for the characters to maintain it. And the magic doesn't always come when the character expects it. What is even more interesting is that while the pattern is found a lot in the Comedies, it is usually in much gentler situations, often in songs *(Two Gentlemen of Verona, Merry Wives of Windsor, Much Ado About Nothing, Twelfth Night, The Winters Tale)* and/or simplistic poetry *(Loves Labours Lost* and *As You Like It)*, as well as the casket sequence in *The Merchant of Venice.*

It's too easy to dismiss these settings as inferior poetry known as doggerel. But this may be doing the moment and the character a great disservice. The language may be simplistic, but the passion and the magical/ritual intent behind it is wonderfully sincere. It's not just a matter of magic for the sake of magic, as with Pucke and Oberon enchanting mortals and Titania. It's a matter of the human heart's desires too. Orlando, in *As You Like It,* when writing peons of praise to Rosalind suggesting that she is composed of the best parts of the mythical heroines because

> THEREfore HEAVen NATure CHARG"D
> THAT one B0Die SHOULD be FILL"D
> WITH all GRACes WIDE enLARG"D

And what could be better than Autolycus *(The Winters Tale)* using magic in his opening song as an extra enticement to trap the unwary into buying all his peddler's goods, ballads, and trinkets.

To help the reader, most magic/ritual lines will be bolded in the Folio text version of the speeches.

ACKNOWLEDGMENTS

Neil dedicated *The Applause First Folio in Modern Type*
  "To All Who Have Gone Before"
and there are so many who have gone before in the sharing of Shakespeare through publication. Back to John Heminge and Henry Condell who published *Mr. William Shakespeares Comedies, Histories, & Tragedies* which we now know as The First Folio and so preserved 18 plays of Shakespeare which might otherwise have been lost. As they wrote in their note "To the great Variety of Readers.":

> Reade him, therefore; and againe, and againe : And if then you doe not like him, surely you are in some manifest danger, not to understand him. And so we leave you to other of his Friends, whom if you need, can be your guides: if you neede them not, you can lead yourselves, and others, and such readers we wish him.

I want to thank John Cerullo for believing in these books and helping to spread Neil's vision. I want to thank Rachel Reiss for her invaluable advice and assistance. I want to thank my wife, Maren and my family for giving me support, but above all I want to thank Julie Stockton, Neil's widow, who was able to retrive Neil's files from his old non-internet connected Mac, without which these books would not be possible. Thank you Julie.

Shakespeare for Everyone!

Paul Sugarman, April 2021

AUTHOR BIOS

Neil Freeman (1941-2015) trained as an actor at the Bristol Old Vic Theatre School. In the world of professional Shakespeare he acted in fourteen of the plays, directed twenty-four, and coached them all many times over.

His groundbreaking work in using the first printings of the Shakespeare texts in performance, on the rehearsal floor and in the classroom led to lectures at the Shakespeare Association of America and workshops at both the ATHE and VASTA, and grants/fellowships from the National Endowment for the Arts (USA), The Social Science and Humanities Research Council (Canada), and York University in Toronto. He prepared and annotated the thirty-six individual Applause First Folio editions of Shakespeare's plays and the complete *The Applause First Folio of Shakespeare in Modern Type*. For Applause he also compiled *Once More Unto the Speech, Dear Friends*, three volumes (Comedy, History and Tragedy) of Shakespeare speeches with commentary and insights to inform audition preparation.

He was Professor Emeritus in the Department of Theatre, Film and Creative Writing at the University of British Columbia, and dramaturg with The Savage God project, both in Vancouver, Canada. He also taught regularly at the National Theatre School of Canada, Concordia University, Brigham Young University.. He had a Founder's Ring (and the position of Master Teacher) with Shakespeare & Company in Lenox, Mass: he was associated with the Will Geer Theatre in Los Angeles; Bard on the Beach in Vancouver; Repercussion Theatre in Montreal; and worked with the Stratford Festival, Canada, and Shakespeare Santa Cruz.

Paul Sugarman is an actor, editor, writer, and teacher of Shakespeare. He is founder of the Instant Shakespeare Company, which has presented annual readings of all of Shakespeare's plays in New York City for over twenty years. For Applause Theatre & Cinema Books, he edited John Russell Brown's publication of *Shakescenes: Shakespeare for Two* and The Applause Shakespeare Library, as well as Neil Freeman's Applause First Folio Editions and *The Applause First Folio of Shakespeare in Modern Type*. He has published pocket editions of all of Shakespeare's plays using the original settings of the First Folio in modern type for Puck Press. Sugarman studied with Kristin Linklater and Tina Packer at Shakespeare & Company where he met Neil Freeman.